Lessons in
Radical
Innovation

By the same authors:
Ten Lessons from the Future

Lessons in Radical Innovation

South Africans Leading the World

By Wolfgang Grulke
with Gus Silber

Published by @One Communications,
P O Box 651471, Benmore 2010, South Africa

Telephone: +27 (82) 564 6536
E-mail: terri@atone.org

South African Edition, first impression October, 2001

ISBN 0-620-28022-0

Photography by Sally Shorkend and from company files

Cover design by Kassie Naidoo

Copyright © @One Communications 2001

Origination: HRH Graphics, Centurion, South Africa

Printed and bound by: CTP Book Printers (Pty) Ltd, South Africa

From Wolfgang
To Terri
Magical wife, lover and closest friend

From Gus
To Amanda
With love and thanks

Contents

Author's Prologue: The map is not the territory!

Innovation has become the economic religion of the 21st Century, but on its own, innovation is no longer enough to differentiate you from 'the bunch'.
To thrive today, you need radical innovation.

Yes, you've heard it all before. Some crazy consultant pushing change, change, change.

Thomas Stewart, writing in his column in *Fortune* magazine, likened innovation to either a machine or a garden. If it is a machine, companies should design it, build it and manage it. If it is a garden, companies should create the conditions in which it can flourish and then let the magic occur.

What I'll try to show in **this book** is that it is both. **Innovation** requires a **process**, management and **tools**, but also **bold leadership**, **inspiration** and an **open** tolerant culture in which it can **flourish**.

But you will find that this book is not a blueprint for change. It is not a "How to" book. This is not a road map to the territory called innovation.

As you may have noticed, most maps don't describe the territory very well. A map of New York City looks much the same as it did 50 years ago. Nowhere does it tell you where the pot holes or the traffic jams are. Nowhere an indication of where your radio may be stolen while you're listening to it. Nowhere does a map of Johannesburg highlight where your car may be hijacked. The only way you learn about the territory of the real world is to talk, and listen to, the survivors.

There is no guaranteed blueprint that can turn your successful business into an innovative business. There's no golden bullet for radical innovation.

In case you're in a hurry, let me give you the conclusion of my book right here, right now.

There is no guaranteed blueprint that can turn your successful business into an innovative business. There's no golden bullet for radical innovation.

Failure. Now there's a great catalyst. Success, I'm afraid, just doesn't cut it in the innovation stakes. Successful companies appear to turn into "serial incrementalists", leaving the radical stuff to the crazy young upstarts.

What I will do is look at the practical experiences of great innovators for some clues to the things that might work in your business.

But one thing's for sure. The more radical you go, the more likely failure will become.

It seems we have to accept a failure rate of more than 50% if we want to become radical entrepreneurs. The really important thing is not to give up. To learn the lessons of failure, to apply them, to continue taking risks, to continue innovating.

But why subject ourselves and our businesses to this kind of risk?

The consequences of a lack of innovation are severe. They are directly reflected in economic performance. Think of the South African example. In the 1960s, South Africa represented 6% of world GDP. Today that figure is less than 0,5%, but year-on-year our economy has never shrunk. South Africa has simply been out-innovated by other nations who saw the signs and acted fast.

Today half of America's economic growth comes from products that barely existed a decade ago! The degree to which this happens has become a key measure of national success!

Innovation has become the economic religion of the 21st Century, but it's no longer enough to differentiate you from 'the bunch'. To thrive today, you need radical innovation. South Africa has not yet adopted this religion en masse, but there are exceptions. That's what this book is really about. It's about real people like you and me, who took risks. These are people who set themselves outrageous goals, almost impossible odds.

I am a passionate scribbler. Open white space beckons me! When I communicate, I tend to communicate actively, creating images and pictures, spontaneously, at random, on walls, flip charts, or any other available surface.

With that in mind, I have left the left-hand pages of this book essentially 'blank'. The future itself is a blank slate, waiting to be filled in by you and you alone. The blank pages in this book are a perfect metaphor for this way of thinking. Unable to resist the temptation, I've used some of the blank spaces to draw a few images of my own for you. I hope they'll illustrate the text in a more conceptual way. Sometimes my editor has taken the liberty of adding a quote from the text.

Sometimes the page has been intentionally left blank – just for you.

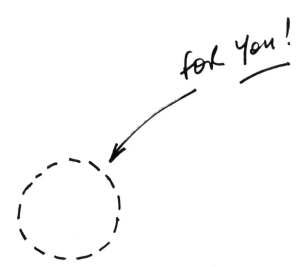

Take a pen or pencil. Do it now. Add some graffiti yourself. Do some white-space thinking! Write down your expectations of this book and re-visit them later. Air your views, if only to re-state the ideas in the book, in ways more relevant to you or your business.

For you too, I hope this book will become your 'work in progress'.

These are just some of the South African individuals and corporations leading the charge into the future. There are more but we had to choose a few.

Included here are people and companies with whom I have shared a common destiny. Where we have often worked and debated into the early hours, way beyond the common sense of sleep.

Here are the stories of those people who have shared my passion for the future, who were prepared to share their ideas and created magic in the process. Sheer magic for their staff, investors and their customers and clients.

Through thought leadership and breakthrough implementation they brought radical innovation to life.

In the end, these people surprised not only their markets and competitors, often they surprised themselves with the degree of innovation they achieved. These are people who set outrageous goals that they themselves considered tough to achieve.

Then they went out and surpassed them.
Are you ready to do the same?

Following the passionate feedback we received from my previous book *Ten Lessons from the Future*, this book has again been designed to encourage you to read *actively*!

Most of the books in my collection have margins covered in comments and sketches. I don't just read books. I actively interact with them! I encourage you to do the same with this book.

Finally, words of thanks to those without whom this book would simply not have been possible.

Firstly to Terri, who was my companion on so many of the trips that led to this book. She challenged my thinking all along the way and ensured that we learned from everyone and everything we encountered. The thinking is clearer because of her.

For constant inspiration and a powerful pull into the future, I must thank my partners and friends in the FutureWorld Network of Gurus. In much of the work we do, we have become one at heart! And hopefully we are all the better for it.

In this work, my role as a Director of the Deloitte and Touche global Innovation Board has given me a sounding board and a laboratory for new thinking. Direct access to their client companies proved invaluable and certainly helped mirror some of our own lessons in radical innovation.

My editor, Gus Silber, has once again done sterling work to pull all the 'stuff' together and turn it into what you see between these pages. He has become a vital partner in weaving these stories of innovation.

I do hope that these inspirational South African innovators will encourage you to be positive, take risks and do amazing things.

From all of us, and all of me, to all of you – Enjoy being radical.

Choose a radical future – and thrive in it!

Wolfgang Grulke
Cape Town
September 2001

The catalysts of radical innovation

The drivers of quantum change

Let's talk about words. Let's begin with one of the most powerful words of all... 'Innovation'.

It's fascinating how the word 'innovation' has become such a positive concept. Words like 'invention' and 'evolution' are much less sought after to describe major achievements.

When someone describes your business as 'innovative' you feel great. But if they call you 'inventive' the compliment seems somewhat dubious – as if your real skill is for making things up.

If someone says that your business is 'evolving', the comment will probably leave you stone cold! It's interesting how the concept of 'evolution' has become so linked to Darwin's theories. It certainly does not appear to be relevant within the context of an innovative business.

And how often do we not bandy about the word 'technology' as one of the key change agents – without so much as a thought for what the word means.

Innovation. Invention. Evolution. Technology. These four words embody powerful concepts, but they are words that are much misunderstood.

When we hear the word 'evolution', our first thoughts turn to Charles Darwin and the evolution of species. Let's start by exploring a few aspects of this 'evolution' and see what lessons we might learn in terms of innovation.

The history of life on this planet commenced around three-and-a-half-billion years ago with the emergence of the first proteins and bacteria. The first living communities emerged shortly thereafter – simple algae called

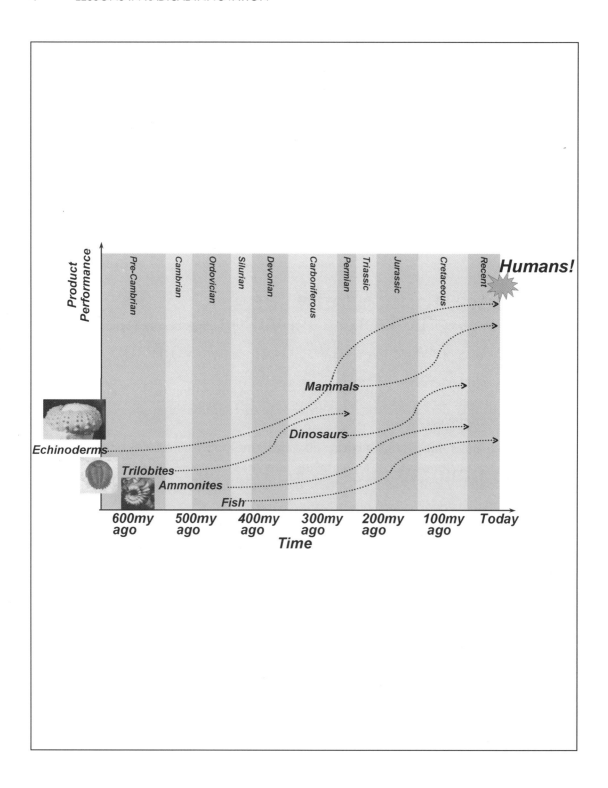

stromatolites – the first living organisms to produce oxygen through photosynthesis.

Photosynthesis literally changed the balance of life…but it took one billion years for enough oxygen to accumulate in the atmosphere and complex cell structures to evolve.

For the next three billion years all life forms would be aquatic.

Seven hundred million years ago the first animals emerged: jellyfish and echinoderms – sea stars, sea urchins and sea cucumbers with their typical five-sided symmetry.

Four hundred million years ago, the first animals ventured onto land, the amphibians.

And two hundred million years ago, new species of reptiles, the dinosaurs, took centre stage.

Then, quite suddenly in geological time, about 65 million years ago, the great mass extinction event happened. No one can quite agree exactly what happened, since obviously no one was there. But it seems as if a massive meteorite, hitting what is now the Caribbean just off Mexico, might have been the catalyst.

In any case, in a relatively short time, all dinosaurs, together with 50% of all animal species on land and in the sea, simply disappeared.

Clearly life on Earth recovered. This was the dawn of the Age of Mammals. Life evolved in many strange and wonderful ways.

By the time Man arrived, the echinoderms had already inhabited the Earth for almost 700 million years. Echinoderms are a spectacular example of evolutionary innovation. Take any sea star from any rock pool off any shore anywhere in the world. Turn it upside down. You will see the result of hundreds of millions of years of evolutionary innovation. A mass of specialised tube feet, highly evolved and highly successful.

Our own ancestors emerged four million years ago, and modern humans, *Homo sapiens sapiens*, emerged just 100 thousand years ago.

evolution

1. The process of disengaging from an existing envelope
2. Developing from a rudimentary to a complete state
3. The hypothesis that the embryo contains the rudiments
of all parts of the future organism
4. The origin of species as a process of development from earlier forms

We've been around just 100 millennia, a very short space of time in cosmic terms. What we've achieved has been nothing short of astounding. This is radical stuff.

Why, with a head start of more than 600 million years have the echinoderms not developed an economic infrastructure? Why have they not invaded land? Why is there no echinoderm stock market?

What made the difference? Why this sudden spurt of radical innovation?

From the first hand axe carved out of brittle flint to the rise of the personal computer, from the printing press to television... technology has made the difference. Our ability to use tools to our advantage changed the balance of power on the planet.

By comparison to what came before, this is not evolutionary innovation.

The history of human development is a history punctuated by radical innovation.

Let's see how a selection of dictionaries define these catalysts of creative change: evolution, invention, innovation and technology.

So, the primary meaning of *evolution* is not that associated with Darwinian evolution – that aspect was added to the original meanings subsequent to Darwin's discoveries.

How exciting the first three meanings are in the context of business innovation!

invention

1. The action of finding discovery
2. Contrivance of a new method

innovation

1. The action of innovating
2. The change into something new
3. The introduction of novelties
4. The alteration of what is established

technology

The practice or application of any of the applied sciences
for practical value or industrial use.

If we look at the meaning of the word 'invention', it's no wonder that we don't want to be called 'inventive' when we do something really innovative.

And what do our selected dictionaries say about *innovation*?

What's interesting about *innovation* and *invention*, is how mundane their definitions really are. By comparison, *evolution* sets the mind racing.

Breaking out of the envelope, creating new paradigms. What particularly excites me is the concept that the embryo contains all the rudiments of the future organism.

We already have inside us all the building blocks of what we will be in future. You can choose your own future.

This is what it really comes down to. The only difference between failure and success is attitude.

Oh, and our willingness to use the technology of the day. But, what exactly is technology?

Whenever I ask an audience that question, they're quick to give me examples of such everyday devices as cellphones, TVs, PCs, the wheel. But, are these really examples of technology?

The answer is "No!" Although in modern usage the term technology has come to represent all these physical devices, the true meaning of the word is different.

You see, cellphones, TVs, PCs, the wheel etc are just the tools that helped us speed our evolution.

entrepreneur

"An entrepreneur constantly shifts economic resources into areas of higher productivity and greater yield."
Jean-Baptiste Say, 1800

Technology really refers to the application of tools. What we do with tools is technology.

Surprised?

Just think about it. If you accept the above definitions, who has responsibility for technology in an organisation? Clearly not the IT department. They are responsible for the tools.

The gardener is not just responsible for the shovel and rake, the gardener is responsible for the use of the tools and for adding value.

In business, technology is everyone's responsibility.

And, seeing that technology has proven itself to be core to human (and business) development, anyone who doesn't get it is clearly not going to be an innovator.

And, what do we call people who innovate with technology? Often we call them entrepreneurs. So what exactly is an entrepreneur? The most powerful definition I could find was one dating from the beginning of the 19th Century.

This may be obvious to you, after reading it. The only word that may surprise here is *constantly*. The implication is that if you do it once or twice, that doesn't make you an entrepreneur. It has to be a constant continuous process.

An entrepreneur is someone who is constantly dissatisfied with the status quo.

It can be hell to have entrepreneurs working for you. No matter how well you are doing, they will always believe that things can be radically different. There is never any time to rest on your laurels. "C'mon let's just let things settle down here," you say. Entrepreneurs are eternally impatient and unreasonable people.

Imagine having a whole team of them working for you.

technology

*The marketing, investment and managerial processes
by which an organisation transforms
labor, capital, materials and information
into products and services of greater value.*

innovation

Refers to a change in one of these 'technologies'.

disruptive technology

Change that topples industry leaders

Clayton Christensen, the Harvard author of the classic *The Innovator's Dilemma*, also adds some more recent perspectives to the definition of these terms – this time from a pure business perspective and in the context of his pet theme – disruptive technologies.

Clayton's definition of *technology* implies that a new technology can be nothing more than an idea – anything that creates a change to the way you do business. Tools and technology are not a pre-requisite to innovation.

Suddenly, for him, the definition of *innovation* becomes a very obvious, yet bland, matter. *Innovation* simply becomes a change in one of these *technologies*.

When this change comes close to being *radical* then often a disruptive technology is involved. In Clayton's terminology a disruptive technology is one that always topples the industry leader.

An example of disruptive technology might be the use of the cellphone. The cellphone itself is the *tool* (remember!), what we do with it is the *technology* that topples industry leaders – in this case the old telecommunications monopolies.

This insight into the true meaning of *technology* is analogous to 'knowledge and the individual'. You are not what you *know*, you are what you *do*!

Grulke: "You are what you do!"

Tools are what you *have*.

Technology is what you *do* with those tools!

Radical Innovation – The bottom line

innovation
plus technology
plus an entrepreneur
___

= A MASSIVELY DISRUPTIVE COCKTAIL

Having spent some time analysing the basic terminology of creative change, let me define what I mean by radical innovation: innovation plus technology plus an entrepreneur equals a massively disruptive cocktail. This is what I call radical innovation.

Radical Innovation always…

Breaks the mould.
The current envelope cannot contain the new innovation paradigm. People ask "What are they up to?" "Are they mad?" "Do they understand this industry?". Only after the radical new idea succeeds do the old players suddenly understand the new paradigm. They 'get it' from their defecting customers.

Gives significantly better returns.
There is almost an order of magnitude difference in long-term returns on radical innovation – 50-60% per annum returns versus the typical 10-20% per annum returns on evolutionary innovation. Companies that budget incrementally, asking their divisions to all deliver 10-20% per annum growth already are defing their future to be incremental. Given that mental model few managers in the corporate hierarchy will step out-of-line and do something radical. This is strategy by default.

Establishes the future norm.
After a new radical innovation is introduced to the market nothing will ever be the same again. No competitor can dare to enter the market with a pre-radical approach or technology. The consumer simply won't buy it.

Attracts venture capital like bees to honey.
Venture capitalists, by their very nature, look for radical returns. Evolutionary ideas and products seldom attract the same level of attention, no matter how low the risk.

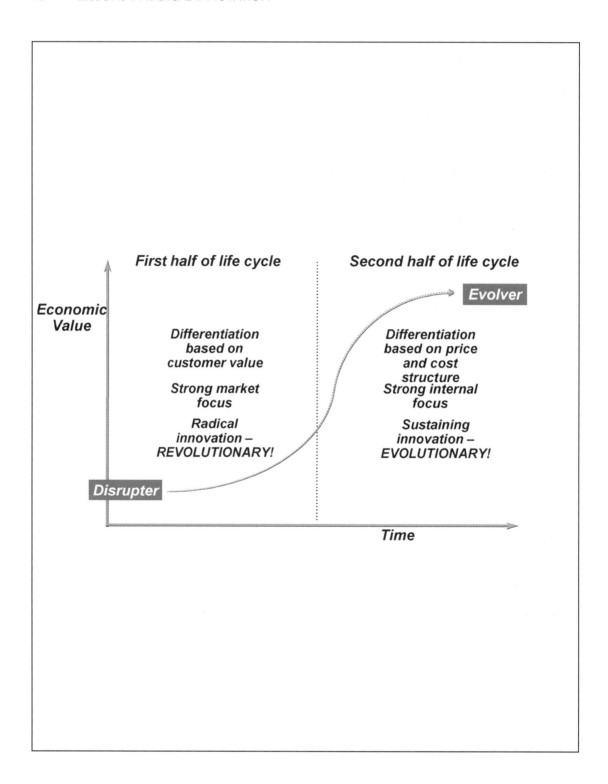

Cycles Big and Small

Everything in life goes through cycles of one sort or another. You can see them in the motions of the planets, the seasons and fashion. You see them in innovation, economics, products and businesses. All of them go through cycles of varying lengths.

The Small Cycles – Business Cycles

In the first half of the life cycle all business thinking is based on customers and their needs. Products and businesses are based on products that add value to these customers.

In the second half of the life cycle, successful companies attract many 'me too' competitors who can only differentiate themselves in existing markets by cutting the price.

At this stage of the cycle, products become increasingly commoditised. Market differentiation is based increasingly on price, resulting in massive focus on costs and operational efficiencies, especially in the market leaders that established these markets.

At this stage, the focus of the market leader becomes primarily internal, and innovation becomes incremental and evolutionary. The aim is to constantly improve product functionality and cost structures. It is in fact the new entrants price-cutting strategies that focuses the market leader into the efficiency spiral and an internal focus.

In the second half of the business life cycle, companies that at their start were considered massive Disrupters eventually succumb to the pressures of the second half of the life cycle, becoming Evolvers. You've gone from having a powerful market focus to suffering from organisational vertigo.

This is where the *organisation* becomes more important than the *business* – in the words of Stan Davis, the organisational tail starts wagging the business dog.

In fact these are two conflicting market paradigms. But, which kind of organisation would YOU choose to do business with? Which business model will win the soul of the customer? No contest.....

Radical innovation
is no longer an option.
It has become a business
imperative.

You can sense the character of these companies in the second half of their life cycle when you deal with them as a customer. The top people in the organisation are in 'staff' and 'management' jobs.

Those positions with direct customer contact are now held by the lowest-paid people in the business

– mostly clerks.

These days many companies have of course gone the extra mile in the name of efficiencies and you are not even faced by clerks but by 'hot lines' and endless muzak.

Can you recall what life as a customer was like at the start of the business cycle? The people who dealt with the customer were the best people in the business, the smartest, sometimes even the founder of the business. Remember the days.

We should never forget that this plummet into the internal efficiency vertigo only happens to successful businesses. The failures disappear off the radar screen before they have the chance to become obsessed with efficiency and lose sight of the customer.

For successful companies, this constant drift from innovation to evolution, requires a quantum shift in corporate thinking, from evolution to revolution.

The state of the corporation at this stage is analogous to an ark ready to tackle a tidal wave.

An ark may have been the absolutely right organisational model for the last 50 years, but with an economic tidal wave on the way, surfboards (small, nimble young companies) may be more appropriate. But, typically, you are caught in the culture trap. You can't recreate the entrepreneurial culture of the first half of the business life cycle amidst the 'efficiency' culture of the second half of the business life cycle.

If you do nothing (i.e. remain addicted to the ark model) you will be wiped out by the disruptive forces of the New Economy.

Radical innovation is no longer an option. It is a business imperative.

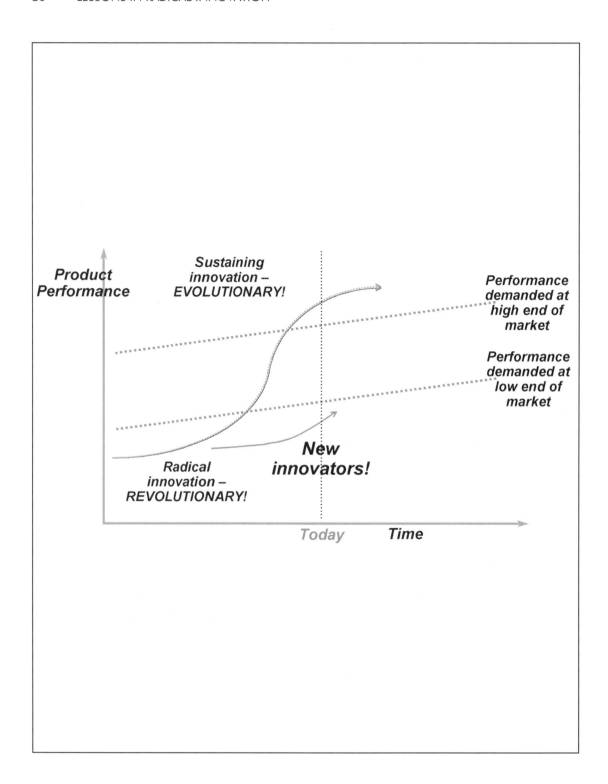

But in the face of these economic and commercial opportunities, why do so many great companies fail in the face of disruptive technologies?

To understand the above, the work of Clayton Christensen provides the most powerful evidence of the challenges faced in this regard by large successful companies. I have often found it useful with our clients to map his thinking onto the concept of business and product lifecycles.

When new companies design their products, in their initial manifestations they almost never meet up to the performance levels demanded at the low end of the market. It is only when their products break through this barrier that they begin to be taken seriously by 'the establishment'.

Clayton notes that it is not only at the bottom end of the market that these barriers exist.

Similarly, at the high end of the market, there are performance levels beyond which the customer no longer attaches value to additional enhancements or functionality.

In our everyday lives we encounter such products all too often: How much of the functionality of the cellphone do you personally use? How many more features on a video recorder would you willingly pay for?

Let's take the example of Microsoft Excel, a product already rated as "too functional" by most of its users. Chances are that you are one of hundreds of millions of Excel users. You most likely use less than 10% of Excel's functionality. Wouldn't it be nice if you pay for only the 10% you use. Will you really value the improved functionality of the next release? How much more will you be prepared to pay?

Yet, despite all indications from the market, Excel is being constantly enhanced by a large team at Microsoft despite

Often, **radical** innovation
is **not**
a rational **financial** decision

obvious indications that the market does not require more functionality. What is really required is a simpler and more flexibly priced product.

But will it come from Microsoft? Little chance. And that is the innovator's dilemma. What's an obvious opportunity to the new innovators is often considered economic suicide for the existing market leader.

How can the executives of the Excel development team break trust by shedding the dream of the world's best spreadsheet program? After all these years of constant celebration in the essence of their success how can they now decide that this is no longer such a noble goal?

Often, radical innovation is not a rational financial decision.

The new products are often simpler, cheaper and more convenient and...that's the trouble...the margins are lower.

The new markets are unknowable and un-sizeable. There is little appetite to cannibalise the existing (and mostly profitable) products. Also, the typical new customers are considered 'insignificant' – the early adopters often represent the least profitable customers, young people, students. And guess what, the current 'blue chip' customers don't want or perhaps can't even use the new products.

Just think of the early attitudes of the big corporates to the personal computer.

How can such a small computer with such a 'Mickey Mouse' operating system be a real threat to the mainframe?

The PC couldn't really be taken seriously.

And, look at those naïve new innovators...the products are less reliable and they don't even make any profit.

So large successful companies don't do it.

They don't innovate radically, even as life in the business world outside evolves and gets ever more hostile for the old life forms.

Even more surprising perhaps is that Clayton Christensen's research has shown that, consistently, sound decisions by good managers lead to failure. Just by planning better, working harder and focusing on the customer, things start coming off the rails.

Improving product features and efficiencies is useless if the products are losing their relevance in the eyes of the customer. Good management is simply not enough in the face of disruptive technologies.

We should also never forget the inherent difference between sustaining technologies and disruptive technologies: Sustaining technologies tend to improve product performance, while disruptive technologies often result in worse product performance, at least initially.

The Big Cycles – Kondratieff

Nikolai Dmitrijewitsch Kondratieff (1892 - 1938), published his essay "Long Economic Cycles" in 1922. This study of the long cycles in capitalist economies did not find favour with his superiors; and Kondratieff ended his life in Siberian exile, never quite having found answers to the two big questions. "Why?" and "So what?"

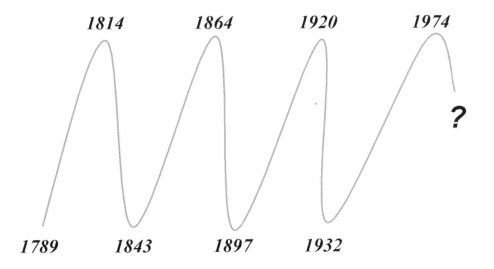

The Big Cycles – Schumpeter

Yosef Schumpeter, Harvard professor and one-time Austrian Minister of Finance believed the driving force behind the Kondratieff waves was innovation, by which he meant not only new inventions, but any "change in the method of supplying commodities."

In his book *Business Cycles*, published in 1939, Schumpeter associated each of Kondratieff's Long Waves with specific innovations in technology and commerce. *The Economist* of February 1999 included a now-famous survey on innovation called *Industry gets religion* from which this chart was taken.

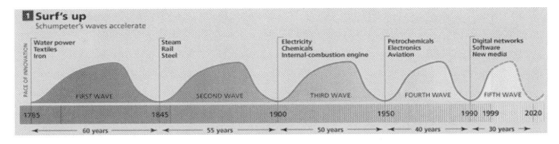

Schumpeter envisioned an economy whose growth was propelled by the entrepreneurial spirit and believed that continuous entrepreneurship was necessary to drive growth. He coined the term "creative destruction" to describe the disruptive effect of true innovation.

It is only now, in the first years of the 21st Century, that we are again reminded of the destructive aspects of innovation in our day-to-day business life.

Innovation is not the result of one or two innovators innovating once or twice. Innovation at an economic level is the result of hundreds of thousands of entrepreneurs innovating continuously over a long period of time. This is what creates powerful economic waves.

Destruction!	Today	Yesterday	
Railroad employees	231 000	2 076 000	1920
Carriage, harness makers	*	109 000	1900
Telegraph operators	8 000	75 000	1920
Boilermakers	*	74 000	1920
Cobblers	25 000	102 000	1900
Blacksmiths	*	238 000	1910
Watchmakers	*	101 000	1920
Switchboard operators	213 000	421 000	1970
Farm workers	851 000	11 500 000	1910
Total	1 328 000	14 396 000	

Creation!	Today	Yesterday	
Pilots, mechanics	232 000	0	1900
Medical technicians	1 380 000	0	1900
Engineers	1 850 000	38 000	1900
Computer programmers	1 290 000	*	1960
Fax machine workers	699 000	0	1980
Car mechanics	864 000	0	1900
Truck, bus & taxi drivers	3 330 000	0	1900
Professional athletes	77 000	0	1920
TV & radio announcers	30 000	*	1930
Electricians, electronic eq.	711 000	51 000	1900
Optometrists	62 000	*	1910
Total	10 525 000	<100 000	

Every massive wave of innovation brings with it economic activity and sometimes spectacular growth. The bigger the success and the steeper the growth, the greater the risk of simultaneous destruction – of old competitors, of old ways of doing business and of old ways of work.

The negative effect of innovation often manifests most publicly as a loss of jobs. Here are some examples from data provided by the US Bureau of Census. (An * in a cell indicates figures of less than 5000 jobs)

Great and sustained innovation always brings with it a fair share of destruction – of jobs, whole industries and competitors, cherished old ways of doing things, consumer traditions etc.

Any business leader who seriously wants to lead a truly innovative company has to be ready to manage the creative side of innovation, as well as the rather more difficult destructive consequences of innovation.

This dark side of innovation is exactly the reason that executives shy away from real radical innovation – let's explore why the winds of creative destruction can inhibit innovation and what you can do about it.

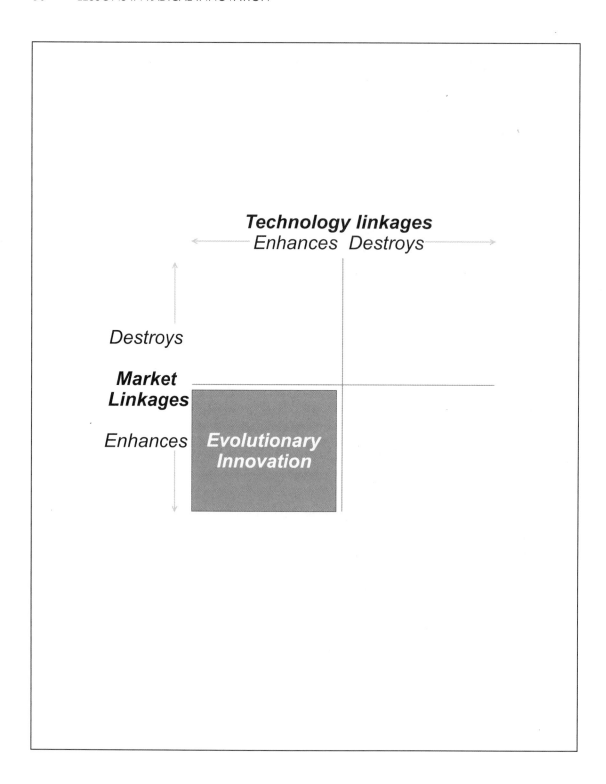

The Winds of Creative Destruction

In 1985, Abernathy and Clark published a research paper in the publication *Research Policy*, a table from which I found to have great relevance in the context of innovation today. Within FutureWorld we use these concepts with our clients and have developed the original model to meet our client needs of today.

The basic matrix consists of two axes that indicate the relative levels of creative destruction in two dimensions:

> **Technology Linkages**: The new innovation either enhances existing technology usage, skills, platforms, investments etc, or destroys them.

> **Market Linkages**: The new innovation either enhances existing market linkages, channels, business partners and processes, or threatens to destroy them.

Any innovation that both enhances current market relationships and the current technology base would be characterised as evolutionary innovation in this model.

Let's take an example to clarify the matrix.

The scene is an **Innovation Board** meeting at a large airline's **head office**.

Everyone from across the group is represented. On the table is an innovative proposal to enhance its reservation system (in which the airline has more than a decade of investment and thousands of technical people supporting it) in order to give its travel agents really innovative new access to services, faster and with simpler interfaces.

Based on this proposal, the current reservation system would be enhanced (not destroyed) and the market linkages (the travel agents) would enjoy significant benefits and ease-of-use. In a survey the travel agents perceived the proposal as "really innovative". Existing technical staff would be able to handle all additions to the systems using their existing expertise.

This is a very **low-risk** approach, creating incremental benefits and a sure thing. This is what we call **evolutionary innovation**.

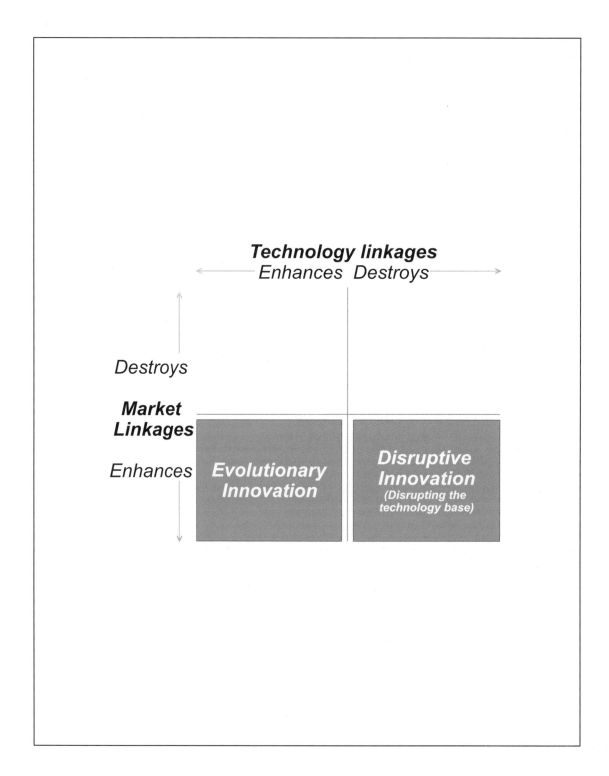

The moment the airline steps out of the bottom-left box the potential destruction begins.

Let's say the airline now decides to go a step further.

A task-force recommends that the 'old' reservation system has come to the end of its useful life and that a radical new approach is needed.

They decide to invest in a new Internet-based reservation system using all the latest technologies that promise to give orders of magnitude improvement in terms of access by the travel agents (Anywhere – anytime is to be the slogan) and significantly lower costs. So, this approach will significantly enhance their current market linkages.

The problem is that their current technical skills are not adequate to do this and re-training is not an option.

The average age of their current technical staff is between 40 and 50. Problem is, the skills they need for the new systems are typically found in 18 to 30 year-olds.

The airline decides to outsource the new development and to have a phased lay-off of the current experts in the technology of their 'old' reservation system. More than 500 existing jobs are threatened by this new innovation as the old technology linkages are destroyed. Union action is anticipated.

When the executive team meet to assess the risk of this new project, the internal turmoil created by this 'radical' step is considered by many to be too risky for the reward of a more effective network of travel agents. They decide on a more evolutionary approach based on enhancements of the current reservation systems. Get the picture? Conflict, and significant innovation, avoided. They have taken the safe evolutionary option.

This approach is sometimes called 'faking innovation'. The inherent assumption here is that that the punishment for failure is larger than the reward for success.

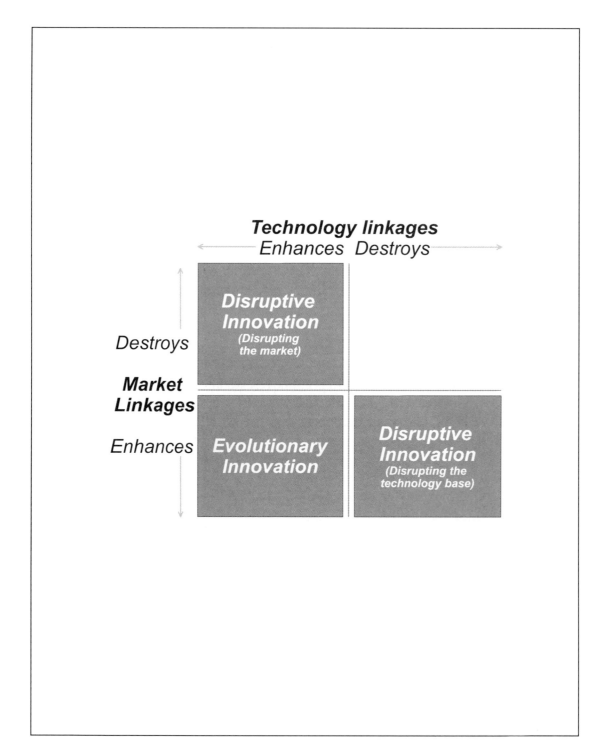

You can just imagine a similar scenario if the airline decided to build a very user-friendly front-end to the system and to make that directly available to customers via their web site so that they could do their own reservations, allowing **all customers** with Internet access to **bypass** the travel agents. The airline decides to sweeten the pill for the customers by offering them a 10% discount for booking and paying on-line.

While this approach would not be disruptive to the airline's technology linkages (it would in fact build on their investments) it would potentially create an extremely negative response from the travel agents. This too would be an example of disruptive innovation – this time disrupting the **market** linkages.

British Airways in fact considered this disruptive option and then went so far as to create a separate airline *Go!* in order to offer this innovation without offending their travel agents. *Go!* was similar to BA, essentially the *Budget BA*, but you had to book per telephone or the Internet. No tickets were issued and the savings passed on to the passenger.

Think about the lengths executives will go to avoid destroying the current market linkages! While many airlines offer on-line reservations and purchasing of tickets few have had the courage to price these lower (even if the savings are substantial) for fear of offending their tried and trusted channel. *Go!* was subsequently disposed of by British Airways in July 2001 for GBPounds 110 million, way beyond the initial investment of GBPounds 25 million.

Now, let's go back to our fictitious airline's Innovation Board meeting.

Suddenly a young executive stands up at the back of the room and asks:

"If we are going to be **radical**, and potentially alienate the travel agent community by threatening part of their customer base that has access to the Internet, why don't we get **really radical** and take away their **total** customer base?"

"The problem with the Internet is that it doesn't cover the entire market for travel reservations, we need an infrastructure that **every customer** has access to. Why don't we create a joint venture with the mobile phone companies and put a new reservation facility into every mobile phone. Imagine this – just hold down the # key for 5 seconds and you have direct access to our reservation system. To all intents and purposes, every one of

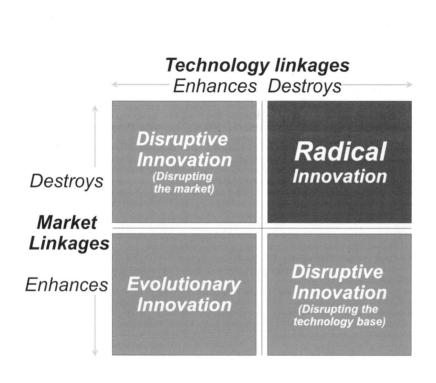

our customers has a mobile phone and all we need is some really sexy software. We can share the savings with any customer who books this way and pass, say, a 10% saving directly on to the customer."

The HR executive ponders this for a moment and then concludes: "But we don't have any of these skills available in-house! Also, with our current profile in the market as an employer I don't believe we can attract the right kind of skills into this organisation – we'd have to source these skills through some sort of partnership. Even the mobile phone companies have very few of these skills. I can just imagine the enthusiasm we'd get from the folks in IT – once this new system is bedded down they would see the writing on the wall for their own jobs. I don't believe they would be able to or willing to be re-skilled."

The young executive is unbowed: "The travel agents will hate us but the customer will see real savings immediately. This innovation could make us the darling of business and leisure travellers the world over. Imagine the ad campaign – *'We're as far away as your # key!'* The unions may hate us but we'll put this airline onto the high road – we'll be leading the airline industry into the future. Can we afford not to do this?"

Now that's what I call radical innovation.

Innovation that simultaneously destroys the technology base – by leap-frogging into unproven disruptive technology – plus the market linkages, by making it very difficult for travel agents to compete with the airline. They couldn't do it on price so they would have to develop really innovative new value-adding services to keep their customers.

This Creative Destruction matrix has become a powerful tool in the work we do with our clients. We use it to create an Innovation Profile for a business, together with their executive team, in less than an hour. This is how it works.

- Identify the top activities (perhaps ten or so) in which you focus resources in your business.
- Represent each one by a bubble that represents your view of the size of the investment and put these bubbles where you believe they fit in the matrix, depending on the degree to which they potentially enhance or destroy the current market linkages and technology.
- Step back and consider the overall profile of your business – what kind of business are you in terms of innovation?

The possibilities are of course endless, but let's say you created a matrix that looked something like this.

What kind of a company would you be dealing with?

Most likely a very new company. Great ideas, great people, great innovators, but not yet a proven approach to market. They may not yet be generating much revenue. Certainly, you would not yet be generating any profit. Perhaps the profile of a typical young dot-com business, regarded by analysts as very exciting but very risky. Based on the experience of the past decade only 5 – 10% of these companies ever make it to profitability.

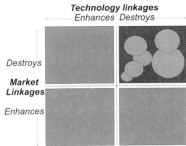

Look at this next matrix. What kind of a business would this be?

Most likely this is a real cash-cow business. An established, well-managed business that's simply not running any high-risk projects. They are not investing in their future success. They probably dedicate no more than 1-2% of their revenues to innovation. They are highly regarded by investment analysts for delivering consistent returns over a long period of time.

But, they most likely have no future. In fast-changing markets you have to innovate faster than others in the marketplace. The above is a classical example of a company that is selling their future to pay for short-term financial returns.

We realise that an ideal business is most likely one that looks something like this.

A well-balanced business that has a great 'current reality' has clearly decided on its 'desired future' and is investing in it.

They most likely allocate around 10%-20% of their revenues to radical projects.

The reality is that only radical innovation builds future markets and ensures future relevance

Only radical innovation builds future markets and ensures future relevance

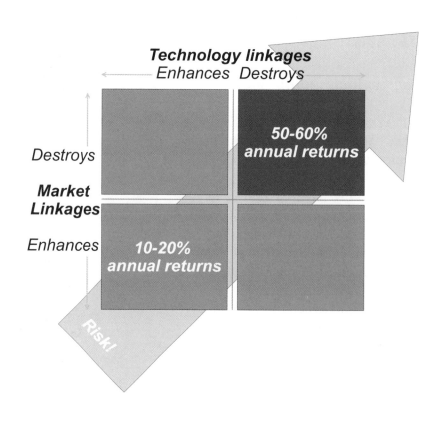

Technology linkages
Enhances   Destroys

Destroys

Market Linkages

Enhances

50-60% annual returns

10-20% annual returns

Risk!

In summary, here are few things about the matrix we should never forget.

1. **Risk increases exponentially from bottom-left to top-right.** Choose your own number for what accepted failure rates are in the radical innovation box. Companies we have seen have had practical experiences in failure rates of anything from 50-90%. The only rule that comes through constantly is: if you're going to fail, fail very very quickly. There is nothing more painful to the bottom line or morale than slow failure.

2. **Potential returns from successful radical innovations far outweigh those from evolutionary innovations.** One company we worked with used this long-term rule-of-thumb based on their own practical experience: 10-20% returns annually from evolutionary innovation, 50-60% returns annually from radical innovation.

3. **It does not take any more effort or energy to be radical than to be evolutionary.** Either way you're going to be busy all the time. It may just take a little more passion, confidence and leadership.

4. **Don't ever put people in the wrong box.** If you want to be a conservative company that is seen as an evolutionary innovator (there may be nothing wrong with that), then don't hire radical innovators. At best, they will be totally frustrated and will not stay long, or at worst they will take down a part of your business with them. Similarly, if you have bred incrementalists, don't suddenly ask them to be radical – you will scare them to death and they will think the company has gone mad.

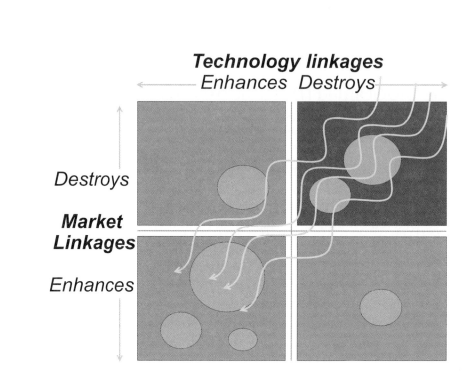

5. **Radical innovation is time-bound, today's 'radical' is tomorrows 'norm'.** Imagine the matrix as if there is a river flowing from top-right to bottom-left.

The bigger and more visible the innovation, the faster it will be swept towards 'the norm'.

Any radical idea (in the top-right box) will, over time, be swept to the bottom-left, it will become absolutely the norm. Our 'river of time' spares no large objects. At best, any new innovations to this 'old' idea will be considered evolutionary. Radical innovation is a constant drive to fill the top-right box with radical new projects.

You must threaten your own business before someone else does.

Sometimes too, radical innovation seems to turn back on itself. What seemed like a great idea for a long period of time, suddenly loses its relevance when the context changes. You're never safe. It's not only if you're heading up Intel that you need to be paranoid!

Every innovation, no matter how radical is dramatically shaped by the rivers of time that run through all of our markets!

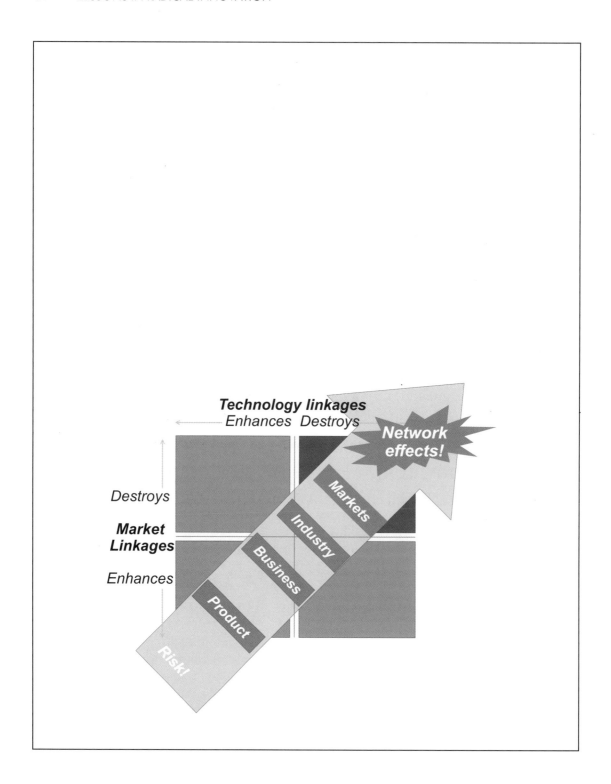

The Source and Consequence of Innovation

From the innovator's viewpoint innovation can arise almost anywhere and from any source. Most typically it is at a component or product level where the primary innovations occur. But it is only when these cascade up the food chain that their real value is felt.

Radical innovation at a component level that has vast impact on world markets is perhaps the most impressive. Consider how a simple idea like tilting the read/write head in a VCR turned it from a niche market in recording studios into the second most popular consumer appliance in history.

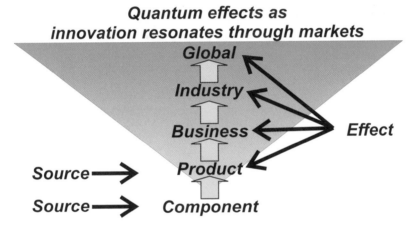

Evolutionary innovation is relatively risk-free and companies that innovate at this level generally focus on improvements at the 'product level (see chart at left) – making them faster, better, cheaper.

Going up the innovation/risk ladder in our matrix you enter the domain of innovation at the total business level, but of course risk increases exponentially.

Beyond this the company enters the domain of radical innovation (in the top-right box of the matrix). Here it is typical to encounter high-risk innovation that will change an entire industry (think back to American Airlines original airline reservation strategy), and ultimately there are radical innovations that change global markets.

Reaching the pinnacle of innovation
is not about more effort
or more capital investment.
It's about quality of thinking
(thought leadership) and about bold
follow-through for new projects
(breakthrough implementation).

The companies that achieve these levels of innovation are typically held up to be role models way beyond their specific industry.

At the pinnacle of radical innovation lie those 'Network Effects' where a particular innovation is so profound that it allows the innovator to draw economic value anytime anyone in the industry moves. Consider the way that Qualcomm has built such a powerful position for itself in the mobile phone market globally. Almost every time anyone anywhere manufactures a cell phone, Qualcomm receives 'A Few Dollars More' in royalties. The more successful the industry becomes overall, the better off they are. This is a utopian annuity income. No wonder they have been one of the most successful stocks on Nasdaq over the past decade.

This is the Law of Increasing Returns in action.

Consider a bank that publishes all of its competitors' mortgage rates on their web site. Wouldn't they become the first choice portal for such information? Could they not attract more consumers than competitors who only published their own rates? Can you imagine how hard you would work to make sure that your rates were constantly competitive if you knew that you had to expose your own rates to the best in the market, on your web site every day.

It doesn't make sense until you begin to think disruptively!

The Network Effect is the pinnacle we strive for each time we work with a client on radical innovation.

We ask: Where are the Network Effects?

The answer is seldom obvious. It is a relentless pursuit beyond the 'One right answer'.

Whenever we reach what we think is the end – you know the feeling "That's it. Finally we have the answer." – we say "That's not good enough. Let's try to be a bit more radical. Let's go beyond. How can we capitalise on more network effects?"

Reaching the pinnacle of innovation is not about more effort or more capital investment. This is about quality of thinking (thought leadership) and about bold follow-through for the new projects that emerge (breakthrough implementation).

The fractal nature of the Radical Innovation

Radical innovation is highly uncertain, unpredictable – you must learn to keep the faith.

This is not just about being risk-averse. It's also about strategic patience.

Radical projects are sporadic, with many stops and starts, many blind alleys – it's the most fearful maze not unlike the ancient medina of Fez.

There is constant death and rebirth – relevance changes with the market, needs are never the same the second time around – you need to keep your mind actively open. Remember it's like a parachute, it tends to work best when open.

New ideas never stop coming. Problems never disappear. Reality is always messy. Never shut your mind to emerging late news. Better to hear it now rather than when it's too late. The cost of changing later in the innovation project will always be higher than today.

Once you reach the pinnacle and capitalise on network effects you will realise that the payback is biological – effects are volatile, unpredictable and non-linear – there are sudden bifurcation points that can go up or down. Butterfly effects are everywhere – very small changes can have massive consequences.

At times, everything appears to be counter-intuitive – management practices that work for incremental innovation often deter radical innovation

There seems to be little evidence of success in implementing deliberate and systematic approaches to radical innovation, but there are many practical examples of useful lessons that we can explore. If you accept that innovation is both a 'machine' and a 'garden' then you will see that we have to explore both worlds – the mechanistic and intuitive.

Radical innovation
is primarily driven through
the 'unreasonable' behaviour
of individuals.
Without personal passion,
the cows of innovation don't calve!

At the heart of these lessons in radical innovation are bold visionary individuals. Despite the fact that most established corporations have spent decades trying to identify innovation processes that can be driven by the organisation centrally, the truth behind radical innovation is the exact opposite – radical innovation is primarily driven through the 'unreasonable' behaviour of individuals. Without personal passion, the cows of innovation don't calve!

But, how can the corporation possibly manage such a disorderly process? The people we need, these entrepreneurs, seem to be totally 'impatient and unreasonable' and unlikely to want to be a part of our current corporate culture.

Managing entrepreneurs seems to be an oxymoron. So how do you do it?

What we'll learn as we share the experiences of innovators is that you have to learn to herd cats!

That's what the rest of this book is all about: Passionate individuals, entrepreneurial behaviour, turning the latest tools into viable technologies and whole dollops of strategic impatience!

We'll meet South African innovators who are leading the world in their thinking, and through their products and services leading global markets. Let's see what they did. Let's see how they succeeded, and why they failed.

In the final chapters I'll be back to pull together some threads that run through each of the stories and introduce you to a process we've developed to help create a context for radical innovation in our clients – we call this process Strategic Thinking and Strategic Action™ – perhaps you'll find it useful in your business too.

Get ready for an exhilarating and passionate ride.

2

Changing the game

Don't just change the rules – change what you are

The alchemy of innovation at its most fundamental – Johnnic shifts from mining gold to networking information

WHOOOOOOSHHH!

That's all you hear to begin with: a low, distant rushing sound, like gas being released from a hot-air balloon. Then the first small puff of smoke, erupting into a thundercloud as a jet of orange flame lifts the bird slowly off the ground.

For a moment, the air is filled with an impossible, overwhelming silence. Followed by the mighty roar of a shockwave that surges across the landscape and smacks you in the pit of your stomach. You're standing on the Equator, at a place called Kourou in French Guiana, watching your first satellite blast into geostationary orbit.

Here is the moment, frozen for posterity on the wall of a boardroom in Sandhurst, Johannesburg. Almost everyone who wanders in is drawn to the image: a perfect symbol of unfettered ambition, boundless possibility, digital technology in thrust. The sky is not the limit. The sky is where the territory begins.

"One day," says Paul Edwards, contemplating the framed memento of his days as a television executive in the Far East, "we're going to have to send up one of our own." Anything can happen. Appointed CEO of Johnnic after a whirlwind ride to the heights of the global satellite television industry – he helped launch M-Net's African service, and was headhunted by Star TV in Hong Kong – the much-travelled Edwards played a leading role in Johnnic's transformation from mining and investment conglomerate into multimedia empire. In 2001, he took on the equally challenging task of running M-Cell,

Media, communication, entertainment... some leading brands in the Johnnic stable

the group's cellular telephony division, in the face of growing competition and radical changes in the field of mobile technology. Either way, Paul Edwards today stands at the epicentre of a company whose primary asset is a resource that is constantly shifting, infinitely replicable.

Information.

Text and images in a newspaper or magazine; hotspots and hyperlinks on a page of HTML; streams of voice and data bouncing off a cellular transmitter; rhythm and melody embedded in the grooves of a Compact Disc; digital impulses being converted and sent back to earth by satellite; motion and emotion projected through celluloid at 24 frames per second.

Media, communication, entertainment. From the Sunday Times to the Sowetan Sunday World, from MTN to M-Net, from Gallo Africa to Nu Metro, from Random House to Exclusive Books, from Cartoon Network to I-Net Bridge.

The convergence of channels and technologies, in an age when the platform is nothing without the content, and the content can't survive without the platform. Control both, and you control the empire. Today, the i in Johnnic stands not only for Information, but for Integration. It wasn't always like this.

Draw an imaginary line between the late 19th Century and the early 21st. Draw a line between Barney Barnato, the Cockney music-hall comedian turned mining magnate, and Cyril Ramaphosa, the trade unionist turned politician turned black empowerment tycoon.

Draw a line between a company founded on the gravity of gold, diamonds, platinum, and property, and a company built on the ether of intellectual capital. Draw a line between the Johannesburg Consolidated Investment Company, and Johnnic Holdings Limited. Now let the line go.

The future is not tethered to the past.

As you trace the trajectory from JCI to Johnnic Holdings, you trace the evolution of a company from a mining-house to an investment house to a sprawling industrial conglomerate that was left to mould its own shape and steer its own course after the historic deal that brought it to light in 1996.

In essence, Anglo-American, the mining and industrial giant of the South African economy, carved off and unbundled Johnnic from JCI, and sold a controlling stake to a consortium of black-owned business and trade union interests known as the National Empowerment Consortium.

At the head of the new company: Cyril Ramaphosa, former Secretary-General of the National Union of Mineworkers, and co-negotiator of the new South African Constitution. Here was a challenge, an opportunity, almost as staggering in its complexity and diversity.

Johnnic Chairman Ramaphosa

Reinvent Johnnic.

With interests in everything from retail (Metro Cash 'n Carry) to property (Gallagher Estates) to beer (South African Breweries), Johnnic was a lumbering, overburdened monolith with no cohesive strategy and very little sense of direction. But somewhere in the tangled web of holdings, was an asset that seemed to pulse with a different kind of vitality.

It was a company called Omni Media, itself the controlling shareholder of a web of companies in the realm of media, entertainment, and telecommunication. The line was drawn.

In the same way that Finland's Nokia transformed itself from a paper and pulp manufacturer into a world-leader in cellular technology, and France's Vivendi built a global media empire on the shell of a waste and water company, Johnnic was about to move from mining and industry into a whole new universe. Out with the old economy, in with the new.

This is a new game. This is not about the quest to extract veins of white or yellow metal from a subterranean rockface, or pry the crystal form of carbon from a hole in the ground. This is about the business of mining knowledge from thin air. A practical demonstration.

Sitting at the boardroom table, M-Cell CEO Paul Edwards flips open his cellphone. It's a Nokia 9110, a pocket-sized hybrid of a notebook computer, a wireless communications device, and a Personal Digital Assistant. "Remember WAP?" asks Edwards. Of course.

Paul Edwards: "We're in the business of creating change. And it never stops."

Only a few months ago, it was the New Big Thing: a revolutionary platform for surfing the Internet and transmitting e-mail via cellphone. In practise, the technology was cursed by its own ambitions. Tiny screens, glacial connections, exorbitant costs.

Edwards remembers trying to use WAP for the simple task of booking two tickets to a movie. It was a classic, almost unconscious case of convergence in action – Johnnic happens to control the cellular company, MTN, as well as the movie-chain, Nu Metro – but the exercise cost him almost as much in airtime as it did for the tickets.

WAP stands for Wireless Application Protocol. Not anymore. "It's Wireless And Pointless," says Edwards. "Or Wait And Pay." Now watch this.

Edwards touches a few buttons on the keypad. He's looking for information. He always is; it's his business. There's a beep of connection. A second later, he's back offline. A dropped call? No. "Look" says Edwards. He angles the screen. Johnnic, it says. 49.90. Ah, the share price, moving up nicely. But that's not the point.

The point is, using SMS (Short Message Service) technology, you can retrieve almost any information you want – finance, news, sport, entertainment – from a dedicated database that matches your number to a pre-determined user profile. The point is, this is Johnnic at work.

The technology is called RIVR, for Remote Interactive Voice Response. Developed and patented by MTN, it's being marketed around the world as the New, Better Thing by Unisys, the American IT giant.

"When we showed it to Unisys," says Edwards, "all they could do was slap their foreheads. 'Why didn't we think of this?' It's such a simple, easy alternative to WAP. And it works. But everyone out there was thinking so far forward, that they missed a solution that was staring them in the face."

Almost as an afterthought, Edwards adds that MTN also serves as the SMS gateway for PC-to-mobile messaging for AOL, the world's biggest Internet Service Provider.

"The data comes down the network from Chicago to Johannesburg, we reformat it into SMS, and we send it out to about 120 countries."

It doesn't matter anymore that Johnnic is a company headquartered on the southern tip of a continent where Internet access is a lot lower down on the list of priorities than access to water and electricity.

What matters, in today's world, is the way you connect. What matters is how you converge.

Neil Jacobsohn is the head of Johnnic e-Ventures, the group's e-commerce and online-content division, their innovation hub. Ask Jacobsohn, a former newspaper journalist, what it's like to work at Johnnic, and he'll tell you two things. Utterly exhausting. And totally exhilarating.

Jacobsohn: "Bricks and clicks and profit."

The exhausting part is trying to merge and converge thoughts, ideas, platforms and media that seem diametrically-opposed by nature. The exhilarating thing is that it works. Even better, it makes money.

"The C-word is like the S-word," says Jacobsohn. "Easy to say, not so easy to do. Everyone talks about convergence today, the way they once talked about synergy. In all humility – no, in all immodesty – I think we've managed to get it right. We truly are a bricks and clicks corporation."

Example? Here's one worth learning. Online education. Start with a simple, social proposition. Education is in crisis. Not enough schools, not enough teachers, not enough money. But wait. Education begins with an e. So why should it begin and end in a world of bricks and mortar?

Johnnic acquires controlling interests in a company called e-degree, and another called The Learning Channel Campus. In concert with a wide range of academic institutions, hard-copy course-material is digitised and formatted in "super-multimedia", following which it is sold online to individuals and corporations.

The **site** should be **more** than just a junction; it should be an entire **network** of highways and byways and intersecting paths of **common interest**

Print media, television, and video are roped in, from inside the group, to leverage opportunities and expand possibilities. Suddenly, Johnnic is in the teaching and learning business: "Primary, secondary, tertiary, adult basic, continuing professional education…the whole thing, soup to nuts," says Edwards.

In the same way, ever-inquisitive, ever-acquisitive, Johnnic acquires control of an online employment agency called Career Junction. At first, it's nothing but a plain-text listing of Positions Wanted and Positions Vacant.

"Totally useless," says Edwards. Someone suggests that the site should be more than just a junction; it should be an entire network of highways and byways and intersecting paths of common interest. It should be a community. So that's what it becomes. Go to today, and you'll see a working template of an economy talking to itself.

CareerSeekers, Recruiters, Online Resumes, career advice, e-mail job alerts. Combine it with the power of the Sunday Times Appointments Section, join forces with a selection of leading employment agencies, and what have you got? Something rare, precious, and radically different to the rest.

"A dot.com," says Edwards, "that makes money."

In the face of the digital economy meltdown, in a world where e-commerce has become a synonym for money down the drain, Johnnic has figured out the slap-on-the-forehead formula for success. Information doesn't need to be free.

Only four per cent of Johnnic's online ventures are consumer-based; the rest are strictly B2B. But this is where the C-word comes in again. Converge, merge, emerge. In the Johnnic empire, online and offline, real and virtual, bricks and clicks, are merely flip-sides of the same coin. Everything aligns, everything fits, everything snaps into place.

Go to see a movie at Nu Metro, buy the soundtrack on Gallo, get the book on Random House at Exclusive Books, enter the competition on M-Net, read the review in the Sunday Times, visit the website, send your friend an SMS on MTN, go to see the next movie together. The beauty of it is, you probably won't even realise you're converging.

"You have to look beyond the medium," says Jacobsohn. "You have to focus on the bigger picture."

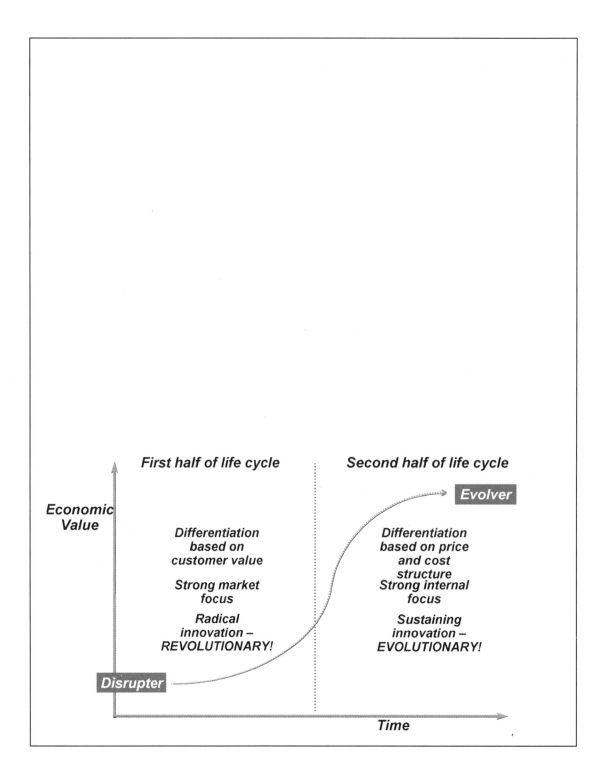

He name-drops Marshall McLuhan, the Canadian communications theorist who famously declared that the medium itself was the message: that television and other electronic media would have a far greater impact on society than the messages they conveyed. Of course, he got it wrong.

"The medium isn't the message anymore," says Jacobsohn. A pause for effect. "The modem is the message."

For a newspaperman who still loves the texture and tone of an age-old medium you can fold in two and read in the bath, that's quite an admission to make. But the real question isn't which medium is better than the other when it comes to getting the message across. The real question is: what line of business is Johnnic in, exactly? Telecommunication? Entertainment? Publishing? E-commerce?

Edwards knows the answer. "We've really become a knowledge business," he says. "Part of our secret is focus, and part of our focus is constantly asking ourselves, 'What do we really do? What are our real strengths?' The answer to the second part is great brands, great content, and smart people. The answer to the first part is the way we put it all together. We've got the content, and we've got the capability to deliver."

Edwards: "No limit to what you can do."

At the same time, Johnnic is all too aware that the real business of business is business. Too many New Economy companies make the mistake of getting caught up in their own propaganda, forgetting what Jacobsohn calls the "old-fashioned business metrics" of cost-cutting, streamlining, and efficiency. In effect, you have to be in the first and second half of the business life-cycle at the same time.

At Johnnic, it's all part of the metamorphosis from industrial giant to lean, mean knowledge-machine. By selling non-core assets, consolidating head office structures, getting rid of passive shareholdings and pulling the plug on poor performers, the Group managed to transform a R4 billion debt into R3 billion cash in less than two years.

The Johnnic formula: "Great brands, great content, great people."

That kind of turnaround leaves little tolerance for failure, and the Group has developed a reputation for quickly cutting its losses when all other avenues have been exhausted. Edwards uses Sportsday, the sports-crazy tabloid that was shut down in 1999, as a prime example.

"They just weren't getting anywhere with the circulation," he says, "so I told them to go away, and tell me what we could do to get this to break even. They came back with a business plan that had the paper breaking even in year nine. I said, 'Year nine? You've got to be crazy!' They said, that's how long newspapers take to break even. I said, not anymore they don't.

"Inevitably, there will be failures. You've got to accept that, and you've got to know when to cut and run.

We don't lay blame, we don't sit around whipping ourselves. The good people, you try to re-deploy, and you hope they come up with more ideas. Everyone makes mistakes. The important thing is whether people are enthusiastic, whether they are capable of embracing change. Because that's what we do. We're in the business of creating change. And it never stops."

But if there's one thing Edwards is really proud of, it's turning the Group into a Group: eliminating many of the layers, structures, and hierarchies that kept people hermetically-sealed from each other in what was supposed to be an integrated, single-minded business.

"The worst thing about vertical hierarchies is that they separate you from the coalface. If I'm sitting in a board meeting, and I need to make a decision, I need to know what's happening in that business. The only way you can do that, is by interacting with the management. It works both ways. You can move a lot faster if everyone understands the game. The ideas tend to bubble up a lot quicker, and it's just a nicer environment when you strip out all the layers."

But the shift towards a group ethos at Johnnic has led to benefits that run a lot deeper than communal warmth and fuzziness. Here's just one: accidental innovation.

"If you keep combing through the organisation," says Edwards, "it's amazing how much money you can save as you go deeper and deeper. But at the same time, even if you aren't looking for opportunities, they just keep popping out at you.

The i in Johnnic now stands for information and integration

"A simple cost-saving exercise can turn into a whole new business opportunity. This is our future."

Internal entrepreneurship; external connections. The web keeps spreading. Through its assorted multimedia divisions, Johnnic has built partnerships and working relationships with some of the world's leading media and technology companies. Bertelsman; Vivendi; AOL; Time-Warner.

"What excites me the most, is the fact that what we're doing down here, is what guys are still trying to do in Europe and America. There's none of the 10-year-lag anymore. The stuff we're doing, the technology we're producing, is leading-edge. We're at the forefront. We're connected."

Draw a line between yesterday and tomorrow. Draw a line between a stick of dynamite blasting a hole in a the earth, and a satellite blasting into the stratosphere. Draw a line in the sky, and call it the beginning and end of your territory. Now, get ready to cross it.

"There's no limit," says Edwards, "to what you can do and where you can go when your business is built on information.

As long as you've got enough pipes, as long as you can move it through the air, it's a much more exciting proposition than having to haul something out of the ground."

MY LESSONS LEARNT ?

Lessons Learnt

The future is not tethered to the past

Don't focus so far into the future,
that you miss the opportunities staring you in the face!

The future is about mining knowledge from thin air

Information doesn't necessarily need to be free

Converge: Everything aligns, everything fits,
everything snaps into place

If you have a 'Group', run it as a group, or break it up

What matters in today's world is the way you connect

Link internal entrepreneurship and external connections
– keep the web spreading

If you're going to fail, fail quickly

The business of creating change never stops

3

Eating yourself

A blueprint for cannibalising your own business

How Standard Bank is using bluebean.com as its Trojan Horse to explore new business innovations and delight customers

At the lower end of Simmonds Street, Johannesburg, where the mists of early morning mingle with the fumes of passing traffic, a daily ritual draws to a close as the clock ticks closer to 8am.

Small clusters of people, basking in the sunshine that dapples the concrete walls, take their last puffs of tobacco, fold their newspapers under their arms, and begin streaming into the two sprawling buildings that straddle each side of the road.

At the headquarters of the Standard Bank Investment Corporation, South Africa's biggest bank by measure of assets, another working day has begun.

Within this **solid fortress**, through the **whirring** of **banknotes** and the weighing of **coins**, through electronic impulses that flow through the wires, through columns of figures on spreadsheets and ledgers, **the wheels of an economy** turn.

Money makes money, capital is stockpiled, every transaction is noted and tallied with interest. Built on the pillars of Trust, Security, Integrity, and Discretion, the bank goes about its business in a world of bricks and mortar, much as it has been going about its business for the last 140 years.

But in an office on the shady side of Simmonds Street, behind an unmarked door, a revolution is about to begin.

A task team of 121 people, made up of Internet consultants from the Chicago-based MarchFirst Group, along with a hand-picked selection of

Simpler. Better. Faster.

Standard Bank websites…connecting brands, products and customers

Marketing and Information Technology staff from Standard Bank, is working on a project so secret, that even its codename is barely whispered outside the executive boardroom.

Oceans away, in the city of Minsk, capital of the independent republic of Belarus, 25 of the world's best computer programmers have been roped in on the project.

Their specialty: Java, the language of cross-platform applications on the World Wide Web. It is March, 2000.

The project team – we will call them Brand.Com – have just been informed that they have six months until date of delivery. Six months to fulfil their primary objective: the cannibalisation of Standard Bank. Let us go back to January of the same year.

Peter Wharton-Hood, whose title at the time is director of group technology and e-commerce, has just completed a strategic business presentation to the Board. He has called it "Eat, or be Eaten".

Other banks, warns Wharton-Hood, other institutions, leaner, meaner, hungrier, are circling Standard Bank's customer base, looking for prospects, looking for pickings. The only way to fight them off, is to compete. Better products, better prices, more innovative uses of technology. But external competition is no longer enough.

Wharton-Hood: "Leaner, meaner, hungrier."

Today, you have to compete against yourself, even if it means taking business away from existing, profitable divisions. Today, you have to eat, or be eaten.

What Wharton-Hood is talking about is a new business, a new banking channel, that could generate significant revenue for the bank over time, but will initially compete for custom against Standard Bank Retail.

The presentation goes down like a lead balloon, especially since Wharton-Hood is not simply talking in the abstract. In that crowded room across the road, where people sit huddled over computers, programming, planning, conjuring up a secret business out of untested assumptions and lines of binary code, lies the future of a project that will cost the bank R165 million over the first three years alone.

What is Brand.Com? Nobody knows for sure. Even Wharton-Hood, boyishly, bullishly enthusiastic on the surface, is not getting quite as much sleep as he used to. It's not just the prospect of cannibalisation. It's the prospect of war. Already, the enemy is at the gates.

Nedcor, South Africa's fourth-largest bank, is proceeding with a hostile takeover bid against the Standard Bank Investment Corporation. It is the biggest such bid in the nation's banking history. An offer of R30 billion is on the table.

If 90 per cent of Standard's shareholders accept, and if Government doesn't crush the deal, Standard Bank as an entity will cease to exist. Thousands of employees will lose their jobs. Blue, the colour of the sky, the colour of Standard Bank, will give way to the colour of money, the colour of Nedcor. To the victor will go the spoils. Bye-bye, Brand.Com.

Fast-forward to 2001. Peter Wharton-Hood is sitting in his office in Simmonds Street. He is wearing a blue shirt. Pure coincidence.

At the height of the war, when every Standard Bank teller was wearing a blue tee-shirt emblazoned with the slogan HANDS OFF OUR BANK on Casual Friday, Wharton-Hood once arrived at the office with his hair dyed blue. These are more even-tempered times. But still, it is hard not to let the colour go to your head.

Wharton-Hood is leaning forward in his chair, holding what appears to be a bean between his thumb and forefinger.

It is small, sky-blue, and as Wharton-Hood is quick to point out, entirely edible.

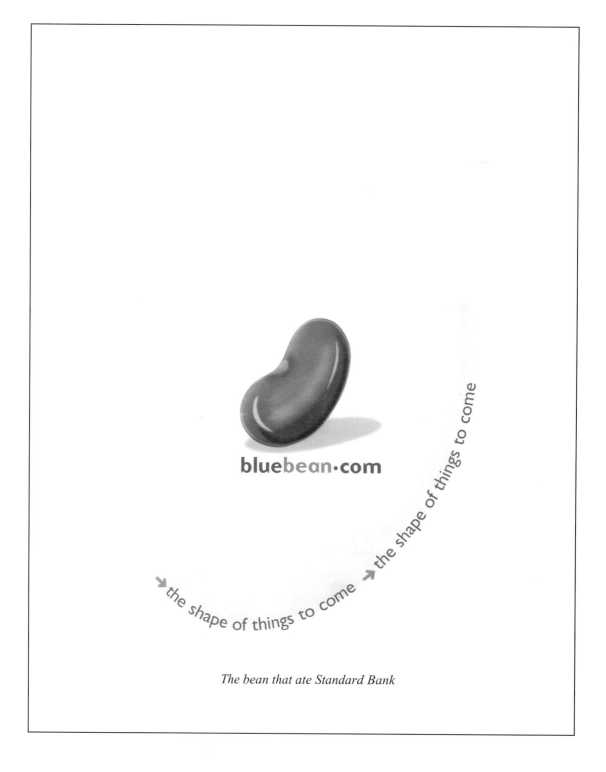

bluebean·com

the shape of things to come the shape of things to come

The bean that ate Standard Bank

"You know what people say about the bean?" he says. "They say the bean is…"

He hesitates for a moment, as if he's not sure whether a banker is allowed to say the word.

"They say the bean is sexy."

He shrugs. Who is he to argue? He puts the bean back in its bowl. This, then, is what became of Brand.Com.

This is the bean that ate Standard Bank. Bluebean.com.

In the beginning, it wasn't even a bean.

It was just the seed of an idea:
a bank without branches, a bank without walls,
a bank that didn't look and feel like a bank.

It would be…well, this is where things begin to get complicated.

An active online community, complete with call-centre; an alternative channel for electronic transaction; a secure vehicle for business-to-consumer e-commerce; a credit card backed by Mastercard; an ATM card, a loyalty card, a garage card, an online shopping card; a full financial services portal, phased in gradually and in partnership with other leading providers.

All these things, integrated, seamless, indivisible, fused into one at the point where – as the catchphrase would have it – "Web Meets World". But more than that, as the project's original codename suggests, bluebean.com would be a Brand. Fully-owned and powered by Standard Bank, but with an image, identity, and territorial imperative of its own.

The target customer would be young (25 to 35), Internet-savvy, restless, discerning, inherently suspicious of traditional institutions and traditional ways of doing business.

Since Wharton-Hood himself falls broadly into that demographic, he is quick to counter the notion that this was going to be a project that would change the world.

"Gee whiz," he says, slipping gladly into the role of devil's advocate, "let's just take a quick look at the business model here. We were looking at a

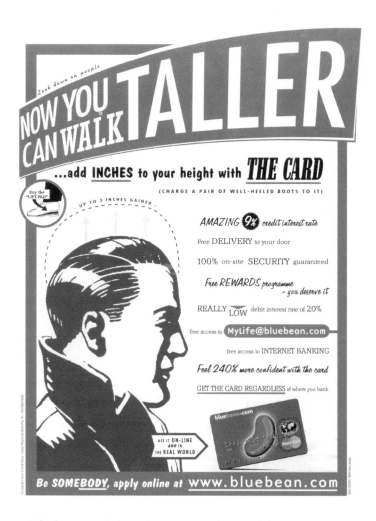

Bluebean.com's launch campaign shattered the boundaries of
traditional bank advertising

real-world credit card…well, there's nothing terribly innovative about that. We already had one-and-a-half-million of the things.

"We were looking at Internet banking…well, we already had a service with 170 000 signed-up customers. We were looking at a loyalty programme...well, again, we already had something called Accolades. I mean, it wasn't as if we were going to be stepping into totally uncharted waters here."

As he speaks, it is easy to picture Wharton-Hood standing in front of the Standard Bank Board, calmly clicking his way through the PowerPoint slides, trying to allay the unspoken fear that the outcome of all this would be something that would bring the bricks and mortar tumbling down. It had all been tried and tested before. It was all going to be delivered on time, on budget. It was all going to work. It was all going to be worth the money.

There was just one problem.
This was an IT thing.
This was a project from the Other Side.

In any modern financial services institution, the battle for market share tends to pale in contrast with the war between two diametrically-opposing factions within. The Bean-Counters, versus the Propeller-Heads. Successful IT systems – networks, databases, servers and mainframes – are the backbone of a bank's day-to-day business, but they're usually run and maintained by people from a different planet.

They look different, think different, speak a different language. Worst of all, they seem to live in a world where time and money are infinitely expandable concepts. At least, that's the way it looked to the people who ran Standard Bank.

"The IT division," says Wharton-Hood, "was seen to be slow on delivery, and unreliable at meeting their promises. Now, they were working on the biggest single project on a six-month delivery date, that the bank had ever commissioned. When we said they'd get it on time, everybody sniggered."

As a Chartered Accountant with an almost evangelical zest for technology, Wharton-Hood was ideally positioned to mediate in both worlds. He made the stakes clear to the Brand.Com team from the start: "On time, on budget, or on your bicycle."

The pressure was on.
It wasn't just a matter of time or money.
Something more intangible
had been thrown into the equation.
Pride.

The pressure was on, and it wasn't just a matter of time or money. Something more intangible, perhaps even more valuable, had been thrown into the equation.

As part of its bid against Stanbic, Nedcor had been claiming the high ground as a banking technology innovator. The merger, it was said, would bring Standard's systems and processes up to speed, for the benefit of staff and customers alike. At Simmonds Street, this was salt on the wound.

"We were being portrayed as technology laggards by the aggressive counter-party," says Wharton-Hood. "More than anything else, that's what galvanised us into action."

"If you go back to the early '80's, you'll see that we pioneered an ATM inside the building, and showed everybody that it worked. We did this against a specific instruction that we couldn't have the capex. Part of that streak has prevailed in the business. Initially, there's always the odd snigger: `You're telling me you can do *what?*' But the philosophy inside the bank has always been to support experimentation."

Wharton-Hood: "On time, on budget, or on your bicycle."

Which begs the R165 million question: why spend all that money, all that time, all that effort, with all those Marketing and IT hot-heads, all those American e-commerce consultants and Belarussian Java-jockeys, on developing an integrated, card-based electronic transaction system that could well turn out to be less than the sum of its parts? A-ha. This is where the clever bit comes in. Bluebean.com, as it would turn out, was just a pretty face.

Behind the bean, behind the flashy website, was a solid, convergent infrastructure that would allow the bank to radically rebuild its entire business across all possible channels.

"The model we created in our heads," says Wharton-Hood, "was one bank platform to service every type of delivery. If you go to a branch, if you

use an ATM, if you use the telephone or the television or the cellphone or the Web, it should all be the same bank, based on the same system. It should be flexible, pervasive, integrated, and convergent. The old infrastructure was creaking at the seams. We decided to build a completely new one, and we decided to build it around the Internet."

It was a neat piece of lateral thinking, as well as a sly way of persuading the Board to come up with the money.

Says Wharton-Hood: "If I was to ask you to sponsor an e-commerce start-up, and I said, 'Give me R165 million to produce something called bluebean.com', you would have said, 'Peter, you've got rocks in your head'.

"But if I asked you for money to present a new, improved architectural platform for the bank at large, and I could prove that it would service the bank across its entire spectrum, over a longer period of time, you'd probably nod your head and say, 'Fine'. That's why we managed to get so much money."

That was just the easy part. Now, Brand.Com had to come up with the goods. Under the day-to-day leadership of Dave Parratt, a specialist in electronic banking and "non-branch" delivery, the team soldiered on in the face of a common enemy. It wasn't just Nedcor, with its plan to swallow the bank whole; it was the very real prospect that other banks, with other integrated products, would beat Standard to the finish-line.

"We knew what our competitors were doing, almost on a daily basis," says Wharton-Hood. "And we knew that they didn't have a clue what we were doing.

"When we saw an analyst's report that said Standard Bank was going nowhere with its e-commerce plans, we knew we were on the right track."

The Nedcor bid may have served as a handy smokescreen, but the whole "go-to-market proposition" of bluebean.com, as Wharton-Hood puts it, was based on mystique. It had to have the aura of something new, something unconventional, something unexpected. You weren't supposed to be able to figure it all out in one go. You were going to have to experience it.

If there was a model for the buzz bluebean.com wanted to create, it had to be Egg in the UK: a bankless bank, powered by the venerable Prudential plc., with a powerful online presence, a range of products that included insurance,

Is it a credit card? Is it a loyalty scheme?
Is it an online shopping passport?

home loans, and investments, and a cocky attitude that kicked off with an indisputable premise: "Life's too short to stand in queues."

Bluebean.com hoped to cash in on that mindset, by going as far as delivering your card to your door. You wouldn't even need to walk into a bank. Aside from sheer convenience, the big attraction would be security: using Standard Bank's Secure Electronic Payment (SEP) facility, you would make your online purchases through the mechanism of direct transfer, without the need to reveal personal information at any stage of the transaction.

While the project had the full backing of the Standard Bank Board, there was one inviolate rule of engagement when it came to marketing the new product.

"We were not going to be allowed to promote the conversion of existing Standard Bank customers to bluebean.com," says Wharton-Hood. "We were going to have to go out there and fight on our own. If we were able to win them over fair and square, that was fine."

With or without direct promotion, Wharton-Hood believed at least 75 per cent of bluebean.com's customers would be lured from the retail division of the bank. That's a big chunk of cannibalisation.

"The comfort factor that had sat in this bank for 140 years, suddenly began to look distinctly uncomfortable. The discomfort was that you had a 121-person, CEO-sponsored project team, out there to make a name for themselves, with a big wallet and a big opportunity."

Wharton-Hood smiles at the memory.

"We got to this point after a meeting at the Rosebank Hyatt where 150 managers from across the business committed themselves to a complete customer-centric focus for the first time in our history.

"We had the head of Retail banking, the head of Retail lending, and the head of Retail's transaction products, all sitting on the board of the project incubator, physically watching the creation of a business model that would take away some of the revenues of their own domain. But there's nothing wrong with a little in-house competition, as long as the customer benefits from the war."

On June 22, 2000, exactly two months before the scheduled launch of Brand.Com, Finance Minister Trevor Manuel rose in the House of Assembly in Cape Town. He had a special announcement to make. The proposed

merger between Nedcor and Standard Bank Investment Corporation, the biggest corporate takeover in South African history, could not be approved by Government.

Champagne corks popped at Simmonds Street. The war had been won. Now, the troops across the road could get ready for battle.

A week after the Minister's announcement, Peter Wharton-Hood stood in the Standard Bank boardroom, and pulled the drape off an artist's model of what appeared to be the world's biggest leguminous plant.

It was blue, and it was a bean: no doubt about that. Now, the project had a name. Blue for Standard Bank, beans for currency. The board, a little hesitantly at first, burst into a round of applause.

A few weeks later, at an ATM in the city of Minsk, Belarus, a man pulls a bright-blue card from his wallet, and inserts it carefully into the slot. He punches a few buttons. The machine whirrs in response. A handful of notes pops out. The man smiles. It is Peter Wharton-Hood, and he has just performed the first successful bluebean.com transaction in history.

Back home, on Tuesday, August 22, 2000, Wharton-Hood rises with a knot in his stomach. He's hardly slept a wink since midnight, when the site quietly went live. Now, he's got to tell the world about it.

"It was like opening the batting for your school's First cricket team. You're putting on your pads, you're taking a deep breath, and you know that the whole team, the whole school, is counting on you."

Wharton-Hood would not be so bold as to say he scored a six for the home side. But in one over, he managed to change the rules of the game. The market and the competition were caught by surprise; the Bank's share-price jumped; the site and the call-centre were deluged with hits and enquiries.

As it turned out, less than half of the customers would be drawn from Standard Bank's existing base. More than that, the big surprise was that the Bean-Counters and the Propeller-Heads were, after all, capable of working together, and bringing a project in on time and on budget.

Once the hype had settled, bluebean.com would find the going not quite as easy as envisioned. "It's a constant process of re-evaluating the needs of the customer, as perceptions of value shift in the balance between web and real world services. Bluebean.com will be a critical architecture around which future product delivery will be built."

Whatever tomorrow may hold for bluebean.com, there was clear vindication of the success of the bank's customer-centric strategy in the 2001 PricewaterhouseCoopers survey of the South African banking industry.

The authoritative survey, based on interviews with heads of banking institutions in South Africa and abroad, ranked Standard Bank number one in six out of 15 categories. These were corporate lending, foreign exchange, bonds, money markets, retail lending and deposits, and – critically for bluebean.com – Internet banking.

Wharton-Hood, now the head of Retail Banking, the division he himself once set out to cannibalise, leans back in his chair.

"You have to have a sense of tolerance," he says. "Not for perceived failure, but for a slower, more controlled way of getting into the marketplace. You have to have the courage to innovate, to capitalise on your discreet strengths and package them in a product that will work for you and your business. You don't have be the first in the market, but you have to be the best."

He scoops his hand into the bowl of little blue beans, and he weighs them in the air.

Wharton-Hood:
Opening the batting

"The thing that really set us apart,"
he says,
"was a sense of balance."

"Yes, we had this big chequebook, but we weren't just throwing money down a hole. Yes, we were doing something different and radical, but we had our feet on the ground. Yes, we were a bunch of young and enthusiastic hot-heads, but we had the backing and support of a seasoned team of mentors."

Youth, experience, caution, innovation, money, timing, discretion. Mix them up the right way, add a little mystique, and you can build yourself a business on any foundation. Even a hill of beans.

MY STRATEGIC ACTIONS?

Lessons Learnt

On time, within budget, or on your bicycle!

Balance the creative cocktail
– experience vs fresh minds and caution vs an appetite for risk

Source your needs via a seamless business network

There's nothing like a common enemy
to galvanise creative energies

Cannibalise your own business before someone else does
– at least you'll own your new competitor

Build new brands for next generation markets

Life's too short to stand in queues

4

Breaking the mould

From workaday white to jungle green jalapeno

How Chef Works re-wrote the global rules for an industry and created the model of a fractal family business

In his office in the Johannesburg suburb of Judith's Paarl, where the flyover leads to rows of run-down factories, warehouses, sporting arenas and semi-detached dwellings, Alan Gross clears some space on a table and throws down a pair of trousers.

They're made of cotton, with tapered legs, two side-pockets, and a drawstring round the waist. But those aren't the first things you notice. The first things you notice are the chilli peppers.

Red-hot, flame-orange, jungle-green. Jalapeno, Pimiento, Banana. You can almost taste the piquant tang, the fiery zest that belies the lightness of the fabric.

Then, just as your eyes are growing accustomed to the design, the trousers are whipped aside and replaced with another pair in the range.

This time, the flavour is Italian: plump tomatoes, sprigs of green onion, spaghetti twirled around a fork. A jazzy bouquet of colours, set against a deep charcoal background. There is the French look, with mushrooms, *escargot*, and clumps of big black grapes. There is the Kitchen Utensils design, with its almost-audible clatter of chopping-knives, slicers, and graters.

Food for thought... Chef Works' UK catalogue

These are **not** garments for the **mild** of **heart**, the cautious of palate.

Even Alan Gross himself, young, upbeat, and informal as he may be, would hesitate to wear them in public.

But that's not the point. The point is, they're flying off the shelves like…well, like, red-hot chilli peppers. "We just can't make them fast enough," says Gross, spinning around in his chair, leaning into his computer, clicking on the latest list of orders from the USA, Canada, England, Europe, Australia, New Zealand, Singapore, Japan, the Middle East, and Africa.

The curious thing is, Gross isn't in the fashion business. He's not even in the food business. His territory lies somewhere in-between, in what he calls the fastest-growing niche in the fastest-growing industry in the world. "The hospitality clothing game."

Go to a restaurant, hotel, or casino in almost any big city, and you probably won't notice what the chefs, the kitchen staff, the meeters-and-greeters are wearing. That's because they'll probably be wearing what people in their profession have been wearing for centuries: plain black or white outfits, crisply starched, with nothing more by way of embellishment than a discreetly-embroidered logo on the pocket.

But all that's changing. It's changing in a way that neatly encapsulates the shifting dynamics of business in the 21st Century: worlds in collision. E-commerce versus personalised, over-the-counter service. The small family enterprise versus the giant global franchise. A back-office on the outskirts of Johannesburg versus a dot.com on the Web. Age-old tradition versus radical innovation.

Where does it all **begin?**

Where does it lead? Where do you draw the line, how do you bridge the gulf?

How do you **leap-frog** the thinking
of others in your industry?

How do you change your way of doing business, how do you grow your market, without losing sight of the values and principles that built your business in the first place?

Today, it's a pair of funky baggies, a beanie hat, a baseball cap, an apron, a neckerchief or a doubled-breasted chef's jacket on www.chefwork.com. Yesterday, it was one man and his suitcase. Joseph Gross, son of Eastern European immigrants, hawking textiles door-to-door in the 50's and 60's, while his wife ran a little dress shop in the gold-rush city of Johannesburg.

The rag trade. If you're planning to accumulate riches, it's as good a place as any to start. One day, the customer says to the salesman: "I'm looking for a good, strong pair of overalls." It's not the salesman's line, but he smells an opportunity. He sub-contracts. The salesman becomes a middleman. The customer is happy, the manufacturer is happy.

In 1964, a brand-new business is born –

J. Gross & Co, suppliers and distributors of a range of garments that are as practical and functional as they are immune to the shifting tides of trends.

Boilersuits, dustcoats, butcher's aprons, baker's caps, overalls, safety boots, welding gloves. It's not high fashion, but it's a living.

By the mid-Seventies, the family has grown as swiftly as the business. Five sons, one daughter. And yet, as the eldest son, Alan, leaves school and contemplates the long road ahead, there is no sign that he is getting ready to follow in his father's footsteps.

Academically lacklustre, headstrong and impulsive, he blazes his own trail, convincingly arguing his need to explore all possible options and prospects before he settles down to a career. The one thing he doesn't want to be, just because it's expected of him, is IDB. In Daddy's Business. So well does he put his case, that an acquaintance suggests, only half in jest: You should be a lawyer.

So Alan Gross goes to Law School. He lasts six months.

Partly, it's because he's out on the street, chanting slogans, waving placards, protesting against the iniquity and inequity of the Apartheid Government. But the real reason has very little to do with politics.

Alan Gross: "The one thing I am is totally wound. And I can talk."

Looking back from the distance of his more sedate forties, he readily admits that he lacked the legal mind to match his legal mouth. He talks at the pace of a runaway train, switching tracks in mid-thought, drumming his fingers on the table, glancing around the room, barely able to sit still for a minute. He wouldn't have lasted long in court.

"I never was any great shakes at school or university," says Gross. "I have this thing, I can't concentrate on reading. I probably should have been on Ritalin. But put me in front of a computer, and I can do anything. The one thing I am, is totally wound. I have enormous amounts of energy. And I can talk."

As it would turn out, it was precisely that combination – a short attention-span, a restless, inquisitive nature, a non-linear way of thinking, a rebellious streak, and a natural ability to communicate – that would prove to be the springboard for J. Gross & Co's quantum jump into the future.

But even after dropping out of his law degree and completing his year of compulsory military service, Alan Gross still felt no inclination to get into Workwear and Protective Clothing. An uncle offered him a job at a garage in Hillbrow. Maybe he could try working with his hands. "I burned my hands on a whole lot of exhaust pipes," sighs Gross.

"My father said, 'Come. It's time you learned the game.'"

In 1977, a new dispatch clerk joined the small team at J. Gross & Co in Johannesburg. Alan Gross's job was to make sure all the paperwork was in order before the boilersuits, safety boots, and blood-and-fat-resistant butcher's capes went out the door. For someone who can't sit still for a minute, it must have been torment.

Gross knew, if he was going to survive in the family business, that his future wasn't going to lie in dispatch. He was going to have get out there, into the market, and do what he did best: win friends and influence people. As the company's new sales director, he pushed the boundaries by selling Workwear and Protective Clothing in such neighbouring African territories as Zambia, Botswana, Malawi, Angola, Mozambique, and Uganda.

For generations, family businesses have served as models of the best and worst in business practice.

South Africa's Apartheid-enforced isolation made it difficult to push the boundaries any further, but J. Gross & Co was changing in other ways as well. By buying a bankrupt clothing factory in Durban, the business was able to add the missing link to its chain of value: Manufacturing, Supply, and Distribution. Now, it was all in the business. Now, it was all in the family.

For generations, across the world, family businesses have served as models of the best and worst in business practice.

On the one hand, by establishing lines of succession, they provide a welcome sense of continuity and security through the ages. Where there is conflict – and no dynasty can count itself immune from conflict – resolution is often more swiftly reached around the dining-table than in the courtroom.

By tradition, the family business embodies warmth, trust, and goodwill, which find their outlet in personalised service and a hands-on, no-nonsense management style. Decisions can be swiftly made, plans quickly put into action.

On the other hand, a family business can be insular and parochial, suspicious of outsiders, and seemingly oblivious to the flaws and weaknesses of those family members who may not have earned their positions on merit alone.

But in many cases, the dominant negative gene in a family business is the very thing that otherwise ensures its stability...

Resistance to change.

In the case of J. Gross & Co, there was a constant clash between the father's inherent conservatism, and the eldest son's aggressive, "get-out-there" approach to sales and marketing.

It wasn't so much a clash of wills, as a clash of styles. Here was a company that had slowly, painstakingly earned itself a comfortable niche in a difficult and overtraded industry. But for Alan Gross, a position of national leadership in Workwear and Protective Clothing was not, when you thought about it, that much of a big deal.

South Africa was small, distant, off the map.

There had to be other markets out there, other opportunities. In 1994, when the Rainbow Nation finally made its transition to democracy, the door to the outside world began opening. And Gross was ready, as always, to put his foot in it.

Chef Works… radically changing the face of kitchen couture

On a family vacation in Washington DC, tired of malls, monuments, and museums, he picked up a copy of the Yellow Pages and looked under Chef's Clothing. It was a line that made up only 20 per cent of the J. Gross inventory, which seemed to leave a lot of room for expansion. Anyway, what harm could there be in checking out the competition?

Yes, there were some big and established suppliers of clothing to the hospitality industry. Yes, the quality and the prices were good. Yes, it was going to be hard, for a small company from South Africa to break in and get a slice of the market. But you couldn't argue with the arithmetic. In Las Vegas alone, there are more than 160 000 hotel beds. In the whole of South Africa, maybe 75 000. And let's not even talk about the restaurants.

Gross, the family businessman, started calling on his connections. There was younger brother Dale, a "whizzkid" insurance marketer, who had previously emigrated to America and was now working in the telecommunications industry. There was a cousin of Adele Gross, Alan's ever-supportive wife, who happened to be a successful software developer in the USA. Just by coincidence, his portfolio included a hospitality industry clothing management program.

Employees would check-in for work, hand in their civilian clothes, and swipe a card through a machine. A conveyer belt would bring them their uniforms, which would have small electronic transponders fused into the material. At the end of the shift, the process would be repeated in reverse, controlled all along by computers and a piece of custom-designed software.

Connections were made. Together with Dale, Alan met with the sales manager of a major American distributor of hospitality clothing. He liked what he saw. He flipped through the catalogue, felt the cut of the material. He looked at Gross. "How many containers a week can you ship?"

Gross gulped. For once putting the reins on his global ambitions, he agreed to send a single container of mixed hospitality outfits, from chef's jackets to waiter's tunics to maid's aprons, as a test of the American market.

Three months passed. Hardly a single item shifted.

Faced with a container-full of crisply-starched outfits that nobody wanted, Gross began questioning not just his judgement, but his very understanding of

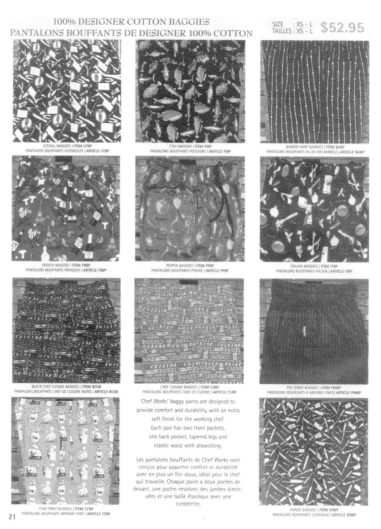

From fish to escargot to barbed wire… a selection of Chef Works' baggies

the business he was in. It wasn't the fashion game. That was the whole point. You're selling workwear. You're not selling something that's going to go out of style or flavour just because somebody in Paris says so.

Sitting in his office in Johannesburg, Gross gestures at rows and rows of garments shrouded in plastic, ready for dispatch.

"There's not a dead item in that warehouse," he says. "You won't find last year's bellbottoms or last year's miniskirt. Every item in there is going to get sold, if not this month, then next month or the month after. It's a staple, like the sugar in your kitchen. It may not go as fast, but with the laundries washing hell out of the garment, and adding chlorine bleach to it, you're going to have to replace it sooner or later."

You live by volume, not by margins. You can't afford to become a victim of fashion. And yet, if you're selling to people in the restaurant and hotel trade, you're selling, by definition, to people at the cutting-edge of trend. People with the power to dictate public taste, to define the flavour of the month. Who says you can't play the game by the same rules?

Let's take the standard, classic chef's jacket, for example.

Who says it has to be 100 per cent cotton, 100 per cent white?

Why can't it be denim and blue? Why can't it be black? Why can't an executive chef in one of the world's top restaurants go to work in a pair of brightly-coloured, chilli pepper-printed baggies, as long as they're comfortable, practical, and in line with all the relevant local health regulations?

Who says you can't look like you're having fun, just because you're working in the kitchen? Already, on TV, you've got guys like Keith Floyd, sipping wine as he whips up exotic dishes in exotic locations, and Jamie Oliver, the Naked Chef, with his wild hair and his wild shirts and his hot 'n spicy "pukka tukka" cuisine.

No wonder that container in the States isn't shifting.

"If we were going to break into the American market," recalls Alan Gross, "we were going to have to reinvent ourselves. We were going to have to get into the funky and outrageous stuff that the

Ahead of the pack... top chefs sporting Chef Works' beanies

celebrity chefs were wearing. It was a bit of a culture shock for us. My father said, 'Look, we're not fashion people. We're in workwear. Do we really want to get involved in this?' But that's the way the market was moving. That was our opportunity."

Soon, the opportunity is seized and transformed into an independent American distribution company called Chef Works, run from America by Dale Gross and two of his brothers: Clive, who used to run a small clothing company in South Africa, and Neil, formerly operations director of J. Gross & Co in Johannesburg.

The idea is that J. Gross & Co will manufacture a specialised line of chef's clothing and ship it to Chef Works, who will get the goods moving in the American market. But first, someone has to design the funky and outrageous stuff. Clive volunteers.

He draws his inspiration, as chefs themselves do, from the things that make life worth living. Good food. Good wine. Good spices. Good sauce. To tell the truth, not everyone shares his taste.

Back in Johannesburg, Alan and Joe Gross are looking at chilli peppers and pasta and fish and mushrooms. On workwear. On trousers and aprons and beanie hats. They're scratching their heads.

Who's going to want to wear this stuff?

It's 2001. Chef Works has more than 30 000 customers in the American market alone. It's the preferred supplier to two major hotel groups. It supplies casinos, cruise lines, restaurants.

Go to Tavern on the Green in New York. Go to Pampelmousse in San Diego. Go to Maloney & Porcelli, go to Rain, go to the St Regis or the Hilton or the Hotel Del Coronado. What's the Executive Chef wearing? What's the Sous Chef wearing? What's the Pastry Chef wearing? Chef Works.

"It's been amazing to me," says Alan Gross. "That we as a South African company could even think of selling our goods overseas. I mean, we're a mature South African business. We always thought we'd be able to make a

living, and educate our children. We always thought we understood the boundaries.

Suddenly, the whole picture changes radically. Suddenly, we're global. Suddenly, everything's different."

Gross is walking through the family warehouse in Johannesburg. He casts a quick, practised eye over the goods that built the business: boilersuits, overalls, combat trousers, PVC raincoats. They're still here, they still sell.

But now, they're outsourced. Now, the full manufacturing capacity of the J. Gross & Co plant is devoted to hospitality clothing by Chef Works. Now, the containers are shifting.

The biggest lessons: if you want to move the goods, try to cut out the middleman. Shorten the distance between yourself and the customer. Focus your business on the things that set you apart.

In 1997, inspired to get wired, Gross persuades his brothers that the time has come to turn Chef Works into a dot.com. The company is about to launch its first major catalogue in the US. Gross, an early Internet adapter, believes the site should be more than just a "banner-waving" exercise. He wants something that will add to the bottom line. He wants a viable, easy-to-manage e-commerce portal.

Alan wants Chef Works to be the Amazon.com of the hospitality clothing industry.

With the backing of his American-based brothers, Gross commission a South African Internet company to build the site. They build something, but it's not what Gross wants. They try again. Increasingly frustrated, Gross does what he should have done in the first place. He sources from within.

The other Gross brother, Gerald, is a computer programmer based in Europe. Websites aren't really his line. He's more into databases. But that's exactly the point: if you can manage the information about your

customers, you can manage the customers. And if you can build on those customer relationships, then you're in business.

If you're starting something new,
you have to build your business
around the customer!

And, build alliances with business partners who can add real value to the customer relationship. Like shipping. Today, www.chefwork.com has in excess of 100 000 garments in stock in the US alone and any item can be shipped to its destination within 24 hours from order.

Chef Works sources its shipping through a partnership with UPS and it's not just about automating the shipping of goods. UPS have become an integral part of their warehousing and logistics. They have installed their automated scales and bar code printers inside the Chef Works warehouse. Customers can track their shipments online using UPS's advanced systems.

UPS began offering their customers the ability to track parcels on the web in 1995. At first they didn't understand what all the fuss was about or why any customer would want to do that, considering their proud record of on-time delivery.

For customers too, tracking parcels has become the norm. From less than 600 000 people checking on their deliveries by phone just 5 years ago, today more than 4 million UPS customers a day now track their parcels via the Internet. Including many of Chef Works customers.

Not content with handling the 13 million packages per day, UPS will now take over your entire eCommerce operation should you not want to do that in-house, they will provide warehousing space and manage your inventory for you. In fact they will mange the entire logistics process for your business. Through UPS Capital they will even take some credit risk and handle payments for you.

Any business, no matter what size, can today capitalize on these fractal resources to tie in to the world's best logistics skills, from wherever they are.

You can literally source anything from anywhere – even though your choice of business partners for truly global logistics is quite limited – you won't find much beyond UPS, FedEx and DHL.

The true scope of your fractal business is limited only by the quality of your thinking.

With this inclusive approach to eBusiness, www.chefwork.com now accounts for some 20 per cent of the company's American business.

And it's not just the hospitality industry that's doing the buying.

"I think a lot of it is people who just like to wear chilli pepper baggies," says Gross. "That's the beauty of the Internet. You get some guy in Biloxi, Mississippi, who would never otherwise be your customer, and here he is placing an order because your site come up in his search engine."

It's the best of all possible worlds. The customer from the Congo, calling to collect his special delivery of boilersuits at the counter of J. Gross & Co. in Johannesburg . The customer from Biloxi, clicking to complete his order for a pair of Italian baggies. The handshake at the trade show. The e-mail from across the world. The real and the virtual. The bricks and the clicks.

"This isn't a Boo.com," says Gross, referring to the super-hip online clothing retailer that spectacularly ran out of steam and money in 2000. "This is a solid manufacturing company with stocks and debtors. We're still cumbersome in many ways. We've been in business for almost forty years, and two generations. But at the same time, we're only just beginning."

The thing is, it's still a family business. Except now, the family's gone global and fractal.

It's a model of a vibrant new style of business: the fractal organisation. Unbounded by geography, unrestricted by hierarchy, drawing its strength and inspiration from a common gene pool of old-fashioned values and service to the customer.

Neil and Dale and Clive in America, running the company, taking the orders, designing the goods. Gerald in Europe, managing the database, coding the HTML. Alan in Johannesburg, trying to do everything at once. Joe Gross, still measuring the cut of the cloth, still feeling the quality, still selling the finest Workwear & Protective Clothing in the business.

Hot-footing his way through the warehouse, Alan Gross suddenly pulls to a halt, reaches up to a shelf, and rips open a covering of clear plastic. He pulls out a beanie hat, and puts it on his head. It's the latest in the range. This time, no food or utensils in the design. Just a few thin, silvery strands against a black background.

"Barbed wire," says Gross. "Inspired by South Africa."

It's a playful jibe at the mood of a paranoid nation, hiding its fears behind high walls and security alarms. But look beyond, and you'll see that things are changing radically.

The fences are down, the boundaries are gone. The world is the territory.

He smiles, and puts the beanie back on the shelf. After all, somebody out there is waiting for it.

MY IDEAS FOR THE FUTURE ?

Lessons Learnt

Check that the definition of 'your business' doesn't limit
your future markets

Focus on what really differentiates you

What is your core competence? Design?

Outsource the traditional business if it has become commoditised

Cut out the middleman

Business is a fractal network without geography

Who says a chef's uniform has to be white?
Question every existing rule

Thirty years of evolutionary growth
can be eclipsed by five years of radical innovation

5

Beating the hierarchy

How the Momentum goldfish swallowed the Lifegro whale, and went on to make small systems and processes big news

On the shores of a man-made lake, in a city of malls, office parks, and municipal buildings, what's so different about the headquarters of a company called Momentum? On the face of it, nothing much. This is Centurion, midway between Johannesburg and Pretoria, where even the most imposing edifice of granite, glass, and landscaped paving has a way of blending into the landscape.

But step into the lobby, with its celestially high ceiling, and its sweeping vista of glass-fronted offices and brushed-metal balustrades, and you begin to get the sense of a different kind of architecture at work.

The architecture of perception.

Here we have a company whose primary business is the grudge purchase: life assurance, and all its related by-products. A company steeped in the stiff formality and brotherhood of post-war Afrikaner entrepreneurship, with Rembrandt, Volkskas, and AVBOB as controlling shareholders.

A company burdened by the weight of its own bureaucracy, struggling to cope with the culture shock of mergers, acquisitions, and rapid socio-political change. A company whose apparent lack of forward motion once seemed to belie its own name. But that's the thing about perceptions.

They shift.

Building a **brand**

Beth van Heerden

At last, Momentum has a Corporate Identity (CI) manual as well as a Corporate Identity team. Since 1993, when Momentum changed to the current logo, individuals and profit centres have operated without any formal guidelines.

By the end of 1999, we had our corporate two-colour logos, blue logos, silver logos, gold logos, black logos and quite a few other colours in-between. It was now time to consolidate and time to start building the Momentum brand.

The first thing we did was to decide whether we should use the one-colour version or the two-colour version as the one and only official Momentum logo. This issue was strongly debated and finally it was decided that our official logo would be the two-colour version.

The next issue that was agreed was that there would be one primary or mother brand, namely that of Momentum. All other divisions or profit centres would differentiate themselves as subbrands using a "banner", i.e. Life, Wealth, Distribution Services etc.

This means that all letterheads, business cards and complimentary slips now look the same except for the differentiating banner.

The CI team consists of Beth van Heerden, Yvonne Ferguson, Esta Calitz and Herman Kruger. If anyone has any questions regarding the use of the logo

on any item, then please refer it to the CI team. We have dedicated Yvonne to assist Momentum Life, Momentum Distribution Services and Momentum Employee Benefits. Herman will assist Momentum Wealth, Momentum Advisory Service, CAS and FAS.

We will have a CI manual printed shortly which you can order from Lizelle Pienaar on (012) 673 7324.

This is the first small step in a three-year plan to actively build the Momentum mother brand. Next month we will have the second instalment of the Momentum Brand Building Program.

The momentum of change… a logo and a company in evolution

Stand in the lobby today, amidst the rising hubbub of conversation, and the flow of people striding to and from the open-plan levels that resemble the decks of a ship, and it's hard to resist the notion that this is a place where barriers have fallen. Of course, it could just be an illusion, crafted by carefully-keyed underfloor and overhead lighting, Zen-like interior gardens, and a selection of vibrant African artworks on the walls.

Corporate Culture. It's a subtle and elusive concept. You cannot communicate it through a logo, a mission statement, the design of a building alone. It's something that takes root and dwells in the open spaces of the mind, whether it is the mind of a customer, a manager, a consultant, or a worker. Ah. Here comes one now.

Rudman: Thriving on change

Schoeman Rudman, with his open-neck shirt in Momentum blue, rushing from meeting to meeting with the slightly harassed, slightly absent-minded look of someone who secretly enjoys being in the eye of the hurricane. Well, maybe not so secretly.

Ask him, as he bounds up the stairs, about the nature of change in business, and he'll talk without taking a breath, drawing inspiration from a mixed bag of analogies that includes the Goldfish Bowl, the Forest, the American Doughnut, and the Tail That Wags the Dog.

Ask him what his title is in the Momentum Group, and you'll have him stumped. He'll stop in mid-stride, scratch his head, take a deep breath. Years ago, when he still wore a jacket and tie to work, it was simple: he was in Sales & Marketing, with a background in contract negotiation, and he was part of the task team that turned Momentum around. But now, it's not such an easy question. Part of the culture here, part of the process, is a calculated overthrow of the tyranny of titles. You are the job that you do, not the position that you hold; you are the blank, boundless space beneath the name on your business card.

Trying to be helpful, Rudman describes himself as a business strategy consultant, with line responsibility for distributing products through alternative, non-broker channels. But it doesn't sound right. It doesn't sound Momentum. So let's just call him a change manager, helping to manage

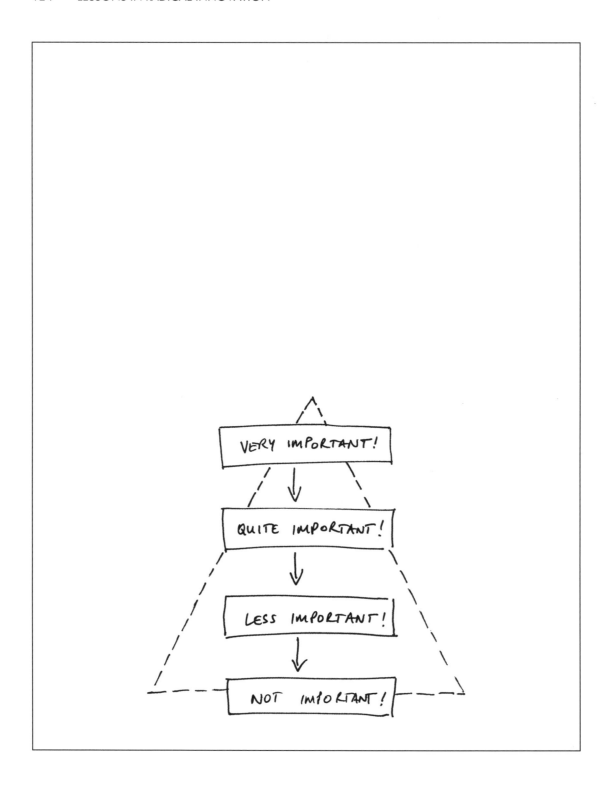

change in an organisation that has always needed change more than it needed managers.

Let's go back to 1989. Momentum, having already absorbed Yorkshire General, Allianz Life, and Rand Assurance, opens wide to swallow a bigger, floundering fish: Lifegro, formerly Legal & General.

With one bite, the acquisition increases Momentum's size eightfold, creating South Africa's fifth-largest insurance company in the process.

But in the age of the lean and mean corporation, that instantly-inflated bulk would turn out to be more of a curse than a blessing. "It was," recalls Laurie Dippenaar, the merchant banker who would go on to head Momentum and its parent company, FirstRand, "a case of a goldfish swallowing a whale, and the whale was suffering from indigestion."

With more than 1 000 staff-members, 400 000 policyholders, R6,6 billion in assets, and 12 million items of data awaiting transfer, Momentum sought relief in the way it knew best: building and reinforcing the Empire: More administration, more delegation, more structure, more hierarchy, more control.

In a glass-panelled meeting-room, with red, blue, and orange chairs, and an equally eye-catching Walter Battis oil on the wall, Schoeman Rudman flips the flipchart to a new page and begins sketching a company organogram. At the top of the heap, in splendid isolation, an oblong box affirms its prime position. VERY IMPORTANT.

Branching off below, three lesser boxes declare themselves QUITE IMPORTANT. Followed by LESS IMPORTANT, and – bottom of the pile – NOT IMPORTANT. The classic structure of any organisation where people know their place. The structure of Momentum, as it used to be. Comfortable. Linear. Secure. But something was missing, says Rudman. Something important.

Another page, another organogram. Momentum today. This time, in pride of place, the name of someone who doesn't even work for the company. CLIENT. Followed, in descending order, by clusters of people who do work for the company: CLIENT SERVICE, TEAM LEADERS, and – like Atlas

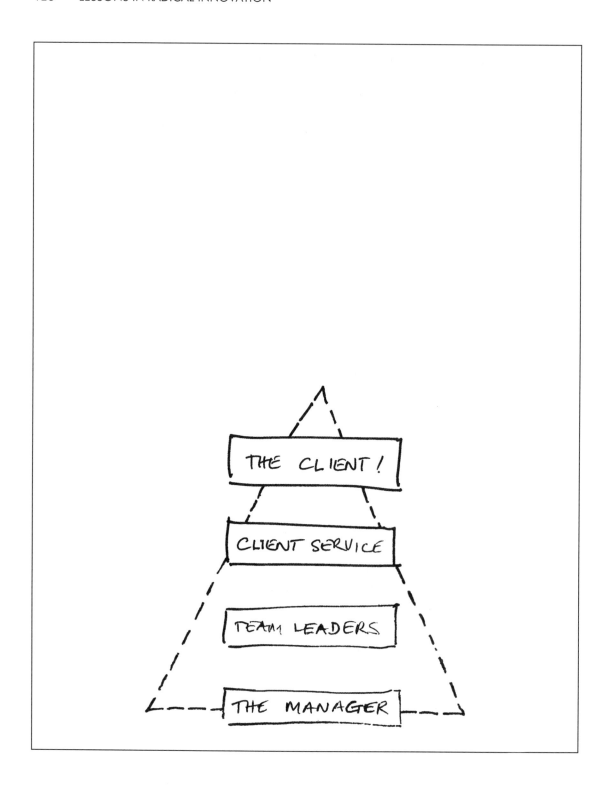

bearing the weight of the world – a member of that now-endangered species, THE MANAGER.

As visions of company strategy go, this is not exactly groundbreaking stuff. Every discount furniture store, every honest-to-goodness used-car dealer, is fond of proclaiming that the Customer is King. The difference is that Momentum meant it, to the extent that the Customer would become the fulcrum for a radical re-design of the way the company saw itself, and the way it did business.

Naturally, there would be casualties. But as Rudman puts it: "The best way to change a company is to make sure that the pain of staying the same is seen to be worse than the pain of changing."

Imagine you're standing on a burning oil platform in the middle of the sea. As the flames leap higher, you're faced with two simple choices: burn alive, or jump into the wild, raging ocean. But wait. Isn't there a case to be made for the Third Way? Put out the fires before they get too serious.

For Momentum, in the early 90's, it was already too late for that. Like every other lumbering giant of the South African insurance industry, the company was under attack by smaller, more nimble players, who were able to offer innovative, finely-tailored products through more streamlined and cost-effective channels of distribution.

The traditional way of selling insurance, as epitomised by the door-to-door, home & hearth hard-sell of the "Man from Prudential", was being threatened by a business model that potentially eliminated the need for brokers, branches, and agents. Now, all you had to do was pick up the phone. Soon, all you would have to do was surf the Net.

As if this wasn't enough, the very shape of the nation was changing, with Apartheid giving way to democracy, and the parochial siege mentality of the 80's giving way to the boundless possibilities of the new global economy. Headquartered in Verwoerdburg, a city that unashamedly took its name from the architect of Apartheid, Momentum found itself in the very frontline of these changes.

But just as Verwoerdburg would soon become Centurion, so would Momentum become... what, exactly? In 1992, the metamorphosis begins.

Momentum, the nation's fifth-largest insurer,
is swallowed up by a bigger fish,
to become part of Rand Merchant Bank Holdings.

On the one hand, an entrepreneurial, performance-driven bank, with roots in the rough-and-tumble gold-mining metropolis of Johannesburg; on the other, a solid, conservative insurer, born and bred in the cloistered confines of Pretoria, the city of Civil Servants.

When the dust has settled, the new Momentum management team gets down to work. It doesn't take long to get to the heart of the problem. Customer service. Specifically, there isn't any.

Instead, there's something called Bureaucratic Bounce, which will be painfully familiar to anyone who has ever been given the run-around by an employee in the public or private sector.

Person A takes your call, listens intently to your tale of woe, puts you through to person E. Person E takes your call, listens intently, puts you through to person Y. And so in, in a seemingly infinite loop of frustration and diminished responsibility, until you either slam the phone down or are mysteriously shunted to the back of the call-centre queue.

Past-masters of Bureaucratic Bounce, Momentum also proved uncannily adept at facilitating the transfer of monies, albeit mainly in one direction. When it came to collecting premiums, the company's systems were smooth, streamlined, and trouble-free. When it came to refunds and policy pay-outs, the cheque was invariably in the post.

Small wonder that Momentum had one of the worst reputations for customer service in an industry where the benchmark base was notoriously low to begin with. So what were the Very Important, Quite Important, and Not-So-Important people of Momentum going to do about all this?

Danie Botes and Rudman: "You can't own the people who work for you."

Simple. Break the company down, tear it apart, build it up again. And this time, build it around the customer.

"The shortcomings at Momentum," explains Schoeman Rudman, "were the inevitable result of an organisation structured along hierarchical lines. Staff were being trained to do specific, specialised tasks, guided all along by strict career development programmes, rigid pay scales, and job descriptions which effectively instructed them what *not* to do. The problems customers were experiencing were not related to any particular steps in the process. The problem lay with the process itself."

Step one: change the process. Eliminate the paperwork, stop the bounce. Establish a single, direct point of contact between the customer and the customer service representative. Ideally, this point – the shortest distance between problem and solution – would be telephonic, allowing for a satisfactory answer to any query, in one unbroken call, at least 80 per cent of the time.

Behind this overly optimistic initial target, lay a fundamental re-think of Momentum's role in a changing economy. No longer were customers basing their choices on price alone. The big proposition was value for money, and value was something you judged on perception, as much as on Rands and Cents.

Were you being served swiftly and politely? Were your queries and concerns being taken seriously, and addressed to your satisfaction in a reasonable space of time? Were you being assisted by real, thinking people, as opposed to operators staring blankly at a screen?

Systems. People. Processes. Technology. Momentum was going to have to find a way to weave them all together, seamlessly and efficiently, and use them as a foundation to support the Very Important Person who alone held the key to the company's success or failure. The customer.

Momentum's lively in-house journal, Moment, reflects the company's changing and diverse culture

Part of the solution, says Rudman, lay in a technology called AWD. Advanced Workflow Distribution. He reaches for the felt-tip again. Phone, Fax, Letter, Walk-in. The four ways a client is most likely to establish contact with Momentum. Four straight lines, leading to a single, central station, which we will call Client Contact.

From here, the lines branch out to a series of other stations, dealing with everything from Financial Controls to IT to Claims to Annuities. The idea is that the client contacts Momentum, and the Client Contact team strives to answer the query or resolve the problem at the first port of call.

If the task is too big for one person to handle, it is immediately and electronically dispatched to one of the specialist areas, which are referred to as Franchises. Each Franchise is run by a team leader, or a Franchise Holder, whose primary function is to…wait a second. Aren't we talking hierarchy here? No. We're talking fractals.

Small, independent units, free-floating yet inextricably linked, markedly different and yet inherently similar, independent yet undeniably part of a bigger, more complex whole.

In mathematics, a fractal is a geometric shape that is equally detailed in structure at any level of magnification. In business, a fractal is…well, nothing more than a molecular model of efficiency in action.

Trouble is, you have to teach people how to think and work in fractals. Even harder, they have to un-learn what they've held as gospel from the day they joined the company. So, when Momentum asks for volunteers for an intensive three-and-a-half month training programme, that will require a 95 per cent individual pass-mark, there is little surprise when the offer is universally declined.

Undeterred, Momentum recruits 12 graduates from outside the company, and puts them through the course. They pass. They get to work. People watch them, people learn. People go on the course. The cycle continues.

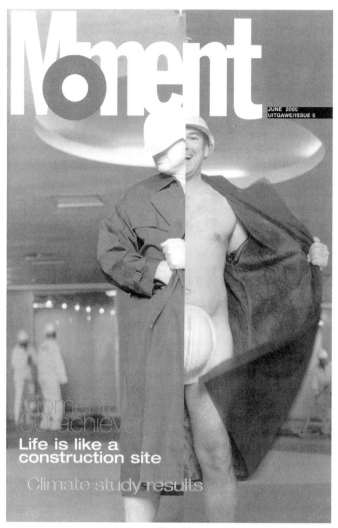

The Full Monty… a flash of constructive fun
from MD Hillie Meyer

Slowly, a new approach, a new attitude, begins taking root at Momentum.

"We're living in a world," says Rudman, "that is moving away from the concept of ownership, to the concept of partnership.

"If you're in business today, you can't simply assume that you own your clients. You have to deserve them. You can't just put a product on the market anymore. In the same way, you can't own the people who work for you. You have to deserve them."

As Advanced Workflow Distribution begins paying dividends, the process starts developing a momentum of its own. At company headquarters, the clearest sign of the gathering revolution comes with the announcement of an immediate end to the long-cherished sanctity of the executive parking-space.

Forget seniority, forget years of service. From now on, he who arrives first, gets the bay in the shade. At the same time, out goes the dress-code that once dictated the look of the Man and Woman from Momentum. Jacket? Tie? Tailored skirt? Suit yourself. If you want to wear jeans and takkies to work, wear jeans and takkies.

Indeed, here on the cover of the company magazine, *Moment*, we have a photograph of a man wearing a trenchcoat, and underneath the trenchcoat, as he casts the flaps aside, we see that he is wearing – thank goodness – a bright yellow construction helmet. Meet Hillie Meyer, managing director of Momentum. He doesn't usually dress like this; the picture is a "Full Monty" celebration of the official opening of the company's new head office.

But the point remains. Clothes don't maketh Man.

"It's stupid to treat highly qualified people like children," says Meyer. "How can you trust someone to structure a multi-million Rand deal, and not trust that same person to show dress sense?"

Meyer, wearing an open-neck shirt and casual trousers, is sitting in his modestly-sized office, where the door is always open because there isn't a door: just a series of three-quarter-size panels on the one side, and glass panels on the other, separating his workspace from the spaces around him.

Meyer: "Away with privilege and status."

"We decided many years ago," he says, "that we no longer needed the old hierarchy. The rules-driven approach made no sense. But once we started, we had to follow through. If hierarchy gets in the way of doing a good job for clients, then other privileges and status symbols make no sense either. So we did away with them."

For one thing, Meer is happy to be called Hillie by everyone who works with him. The days of "Sirs in suits" are gone forever. So, too, are the days of clocking-in at eight and clocking-out at five. The worth of an employee is no longer measured by the minutes in a day; it's measured by the tangibles of productivity, efficiency, and the bottom line.

The temple of hierarchy, with its multiple levels of overlords and underlings and managers in the middle, has been razed to the ground. In its place, a flattened structure of teams and franchises and profit centres, self-controlled, multi-skilled, with each member free to choose a title that best reflects the real nature of the task at hand.

FirstRand Chairman Laurie Dippenaar

"We want 'help-you' titles," says Laurie Dippenaar, now Chairman of FirstRand, the financial services consortium that arose from the merger of Rand Merchant Bank, First National Bank, Southern Life and Momentum in a complex deal in 1998. "We want the customer to be able to get hold of the right person at Momentum, and get the problem solved in a single phone call."

Fishing for a way to describe the new working culture at Momentum, Dippenaar draws inspiration from the walls of glass that surround the open-plan offices at company headquarters.

"And within their confines, you're free to make decisions that work best for you, and work best for the business."

You **earn** what you're **worth.**
You **are** what you **earn.**

"Think of a large fish-bowl," he says.
"The fish can swim where they like,
but obviously not past the glass.
There are boundaries, but they're wide.

The problem, of course, is that people aren't fish. Fish are happy with a few crumbs dropped into their bowl every now and again. People expect bigger reward. In the Momentum of old, whatever your place in the hierarchy, you could model your ambitions and shape your career according to the clearly-delineated scales of remuneration that accompanied every step up the ladder. Now, the corporate ladder is gone. What's happened to the money?

"A fixed salary scale for operational staff no longer makes any sense," says Schoeman Rudman. "Instead, because the automated workflow system allows you to keep track of the performance levels of every individual, it's possible to pay bonuses based on individual efficiency, as measured against the norm."

Today, more than 80 per cent of Momentum's operational staff are remunerated part salary and part unlimited bonus. You are what you earn; you earn what you're worth. Food for thought: consider the doughnut. The dough is on the outside, the hole is on the inside. At Momentum, it's the other way round.

You define the perimeters of your role, and you work your way through to where the dough is. You decide what you can do best, you determine the size of the doughnut. That's the way a meritocracy – let's call it a "Momentocracy" – works. Which is why, of course, it doesn't work for everybody.

For some at Momentum, the new system,
with its new ways of working, its new ways of earning,
and its drop-the-title, dress-as-you-please culture,
was like having a well-worn security blanket
whipped out from under their feet.

In that **simple**, attractive **business model**, lay the prospect of **doomsday** for Momentum's agents

Inevitably, there was unhappiness, followed by resignations and voluntary retrenchments. But for Momentum, there was no holding back.

Underpinning the soft changes to corporate culture and workstyle, was a drive for profit and efficiency that sometimes seemed to verge on the ruthless. For instance, the company decided, shortly after its takeover by Rand Merchant Bank Holdings, to focus its business on the A income sector: those earning R6 000 a month or more.

The rationale was as simple as it was incontrovertible. It costs as much to process, issue and administer a policy with a monthly premium of R30, as it does a premium of R300. But what about Momentum's traditional share of the mining market, particularly in the Western Transvaal, which accounted for 20 per cent of premium income? Would an exception be made to accommodate those in the less-profitable C and D income demographics?

"No," says Rudman. "The bullet had to be bitten. No exceptions. The short-term pain was intense. Branches closed, agents were unhappy. But the focus and the concentration paid off."

He produces a bar-graph. In 1992, Momentum's average monthly premium was R125. According to strict profit targets set that year, it should have gone up to R220 a month by 1995. It didn't. It went up to R380.

But in that simple, attractive business model, lay the prospect of doomsday for a group of people who had traditionally toiled tirelessly in the frontline for Momentum. The agents.

By carefully choosing its target market, Momentum focused its energies on building finely-tailored products that could be delivered through the most efficient distribution channels possible.

In May, 1995, Momentum announced an end to the perks packages that had been enjoyed by its intermediaries for years. Out went the 100 per cent subsidy of phone, fax and postal bills, as did free office accommodation, secretarial allowances, car allowances, petrol allowances, provident and pension fund contributions and medical benefits.

Hard as it was to fault Momentum's reasoning – it can cost as much as 25 per cent more to sell a policy through an agent than through a broker – or argue with its logic – the new, streamlined entrepreneurial approach was delivering results inside the organisation, so agents had to become more competitive and independent as well – those in the frontline were left reeling. The bigger the agent, the bigger the blow.

*Botes: "The edge lies in making
visions happen."*

For Derek Dingwall, one of Momentum's most successful agents – 550 policies per annum, member of the Million-Dollar Round Table for 16 years running – the new strategy meant he was having his featherbed taken from under him. How did he react?

"For years I'd told myself that as a commission-only agent I was self-employed," he says. "It was a shock to realise that all these years I had enjoyed sheltered employment. It was traumatic. I had five support staff and it meant I was losing more than R20 000 a month in various subsidies. But I could see the logic. Momentum wasn't taking without giving something back."

More efficient processes, more innovative products, more intensive training, a more lucrative target market: when the initial pain was over, Momentum's intermediaries were pleased to discover that they could do more business, make more money, even after deductions for expenses.

As the first South African insurance company to dispense with the services of traditional sales consultants or agents, Momentum needed to replace them with a new style of go-between. A new agent, for a new age.

Say **hello** to the New-Age Intermediary.

In effect, you're still dealing with someone who'll be glad to sell you a policy. But now, it's someone with a broader set of skills, a wider range of products, a more acute understanding of the needs and requirements of the target-market.

Says Danie Botes, CEO of Momentum Life: "As the company changed, so our agents and brokers had to change. The old days of being measured on sales and commission alone, are no more. If you want to move forward, you need people who are capable of changing their way of working, capable of diversifying their energies and seizing new opportunities."

Botes is the first to admit that Momentum has no great edge on its competitors when it comes to developing strategic visions of the future.

The edge lies in **making them happen.**

"Believe me," he says,

"**we** are **ruthless** executioners.

" Peer-pressure is a big thing in this company. Most companies have a fair idea of what they want to do, but they're not that great at putting ideas into practice."

The lessons in all this are clear. Ask for proof, and Schoeman Rudman will give you proof until your eyes glaze over.

In 1991, it took seven days to process new business. Today, nine out of 10 new deals are handled within six hours. Previously, 85 per cent of technical changes to policies could be finalised within 15 days. Now, 91 per cent are completed within a day.

Says Rudman: "We saw a 40 per cent reduction in headcount, while transactions doubled. Turnaround time was cut by 70 per cent. It's not just the technology – it's the people. They are now accountable, knowledgeable and motivated. We flattened the hierarchy. Our whole system is transparent. Everyone can see how everyone else is performing."

As it turned out, Momentum's performance has exceeded even its own expectations. In the annual PMR survey, an independent analysis of service and product quality as rated by intermediaries, Momentum was ranked 10th in 1993; fifth in 1994; and Number One for the five years running from 1995 to 2000.

Forget the gold-fish bowl for a moment. Forget the doughnut, forget the blazing oil-platform. What we have here, in an edifice of glass and granite in Centurion, is a company that took a good, hard look at the way it was working, saw that it wasn't working, and decided to do something about it. Something radical, something different, something that rocked the boat, upset the apple-cart, shook the comfort zone to its core.

"In Momentum," says Schoeman Rudman, leaning back in his chair, looking up at the patterns of light playing on glass, "we had the challenge of doing open heart surgery while the patient was carrying a grand piano up the stairs – and we did it. This is a place where science-fiction has become science fact."

He opens the door of the meeting-room, steps back into the eye of the storm.

"And if it can happen here," he says, the hint of a smile playing across his face, "it can happen anywhere."

MY THOUGHTS & NOTES

Lessons Learnt

Bureaucracy is historic baggage, not a future certainty

In a merger, the smallest party's systems and
processes should be retained

Ensure that everyone in the value chain adds value
and if they don't, don't have them in the chain

Make sure your interface to the customer
is staffed by smart empowered people

You can increase customer satisfaction
even while making radical changes

The pain of the change must be seen to be
less than the pain of staying the same
– you must create a 'burning platform'

A fundamental change in business culture
will not accommodate all those
who were there before the change

Innovation is a partnership between technology,
systems, processes and people

Invite people to be part of radical change

The competitive edge lies in making strategy happen
– be ruthless in execution

Learn to thrive in the eye of the storm,
learn to cope with uncertainty and unpredictability

6

Choosing intimacy

Beyond operational efficiency and product leadership

How Citadel is re-writing the rules of investment advice for a volatile world economy, putting the client at the centre of the value network

On a Sunday night in 1993, in a bachelor flat in Sunnyside, Pretoria, three brothers gather round a table with a blank sheet of paper between them. On this **open space**, this **infinite canvas**, they **will** set out to **create** a business, **built** on a commodity that is **impossible** to **quantify**, and is usually **given away for free.**

Advice.

Looking for a good deal on a Retirement Annuity? Looking for a portfolio of Unit Trusts with medium-risk and high return? Looking for the best single-premium offshore investment on the market? Ask Johan, Chris, or Wikus Marais. On second thoughts, don't. Not right now.

This is one of those moments when a sudden, blinding insight overrides every force of habit and strand of conventional thinking. This is when you wipe the **slate** clean and **begin again.**

Here's the equation: as a broker or insurance agent, with the unqualified freedom to call yourself a "financial adviser", you **sell** a **client** an **investment product**, and you **claim** a **commission** based on a sliding scale of term and value. For the advice itself, you don't charge a cent. That's how it works; **that's how it's always worked.**

But now Johan Marais, oldest of the brothers, founder and senior partner of the independent firm of Johan Marais Brokers, picks up a pencil and

IF YOU'RE GOING TO UNDERSTAND THE MARKETS, YOU'LL NEED TO MAKE SENSE OF THEM.

IT'S NOT EASY PUTTING IT ALL TOGETHER. MARKETS ARE INCREASINGLY VOLATILE AND VALUE IS LESS CERTAIN, MAKING INVESTMENT STRATEGIES ALL THE MORE CHALLENGING. YOU'RE INVITED TO JOIN CITADEL INVESTMENT STRATEGISTS FOR AN IN-DEPTH LOOK AT MARKET BEHAVIOUR WHERE WE'LL SHARE OUR

INVESTMENT LESSONS FOR THE FUTURE. YOU'LL APPRECIATE WHY WEALTH IS ABOUT LONG TERM MANAGEMENT, RATHER THAN ONE-OFF SOLUTIONS.

LIGHT REFRESHMENTS WILL BE SERVED. YOU ARE MOST WELCOME TO BRING ALONG A PARTNER OR GUEST WHO MAY BE INTERESTED TO LEARN MORE ABOUT CITADEL.

CITADEL

Trading on the value of its intellectual capital, Citadel sets out to solve
the puzzle of modern markets

draws a line down the middle of the sheet of paper. On the one side, he writes OPPORTUNITIES. On the other, PROBLEMS.

Then he puts a proposition to Chris and Wikus. Let's **stop** selling on commission. **Let's** offer our clients **unbiased**, meaningful, **personalised** financial advice on an ongoing basis. **And let's charge them for it.** By the end of the evening, the scrawls, calculations, asterisks and exclamation marks in the left-hand column outnumber those on the right.

The traditional model of investment selling has just been turned on its head. What if the transaction itself was entirely free of charge? What if you were to pay a fee for professional advice instead, based on a percentage of your assets under management? What if we charged a fee based on the performance of the client's assets? The tap-tap-tap of pencil on paper. The brothers are thinking. Hard.

Johan is a B.Com; Wikus is an M.Phil in Economics; Chris is studying Actuarial Science. Between them they've learned enough to know the rules of the game. Don't rush in until you've explored all the angles. Never take too extreme a position. Don't get sucked into the sentiment of the moment.

The brothers **decide** to put the **proposition** to **the test.** After all, commission is the broker's bread-and-butter. Each slice, each serving, can be accurately measured and accounted for. It's factored into the cost-structure of the products you sell, so the client doesn't see it, or even know it exists. Everyone's happy. But advice?

Advice is something you can take or leave. Advice is part goodwill, part hunch, part inside information. Advice, on its own, is worth about as much...as a set of feverish scribblings on a once-pristine sheet of paper. But there's no harm in trying. During the coming week, without making too much of a fuss, the brothers will put the same question to the selection of clients they've already lined up to see.

How would you feel about paying for unbiased, meaningful, personalised financial advice?

Seven days later, a new investment services company is born. Originally called Johan Marais Investment Services, it will come to be known as Citadel, and it will focus its energies on the small niche of South Africans who have already made money, and who now want to make their money make more.

Louis Fourie: "A company built on the value of value."

"We can't make you rich," says Wikus Marais, going against the grain of every financial adviser's standard opening gambit, "but we can make sure that you stay rich once you are rich."

Carving its own niche in the rarified realm of wealth preservation, Citadel grows to become the second-biggest player in the business by 2001, with R6,5 billion worth of assets under management, and a market value of more than R500 million.

But let us shift our attention away from the balance-sheet for a moment, for this is not a tale of quantifiables or quick formulas or snappily-named products that are never bought, but always sold.

This is a tale of a company built on the premise that the real value of money lies not on the face of the currency, but on the value of value itself. Yes, this is a company founded and run by philosophers, who just happen to have chosen economics as a discipline. Or perhaps it's the other way round.

Meet Louis Fourie, Chairman of Citadel, who joined the Marais brothers in 1994, after ten years as a teacher and practitioner of Economics. As a director of FutureWorld, the global business and technology think-tank, and Spellbound, an education firm that seeks to take learning beyond the boundaries of academia, Fourie is a man whose view of the world is filtered through the beam of a laser-sharp principle: Add value.

Anyone who has ever sat in a boardroom will have heard the mantra, which is just as often recited in reverse. But for Fourie, it bears a little deeper analysis: "Why do so few businesses dominate the global market? Why are so few people truly successful? It's because so few bother to understand the basic rules of value.

"Value can't be dressed up as hype, copied wholesale from another business, or wrapped up in short-term greed.

" If offering real, lasting value isn't your overriding reason for being in business, think again."

In the case of Citadel, the proposition, the opportunity, was that there was very little of that kind of value in the traditional relationship between financial adviser and client. Linked to mainstream investment and insurance houses, the advice tended to be sales-driven, shallow, generic, fragmented, and distinctly once-off in nature: "See a prospect, do his business, hope you don't see him again, unless there's more money to invest".

For the more affluent client, there would usually be a stockbroker somewhere in the mix, managing a portfolio that would be overwhelmingly exposed to one class of assets. Usually, the income would be earned from the transactions themselves, and not from any measure of added value. Then there would be the bank manager, the lawyer, the auditor, the insurance agent: all driven by individual agendas, vested interests, limited fields of vision.

"The fundamental flaw in the existing relationships," says Fourie, "is that there was no integration of all the elements of an individual's personal and financial affairs. No sharing of long-term interest."

Citadel's goal was not so much to consolidate these disparate functions, as to expose the threads of value that lurked beneath the layers. By so doing, naturally, the founders of the company would come up against the interests of a fraternity much bigger than themselves.

By refusing to accept commissions on investment products, and charging for advice instead, Citadel found itself in contravention of the regulations of the Life Offices Association of South Africa. This wasn't a matter of choice: on certain classes of product, agents were obliged to accept the predetermined, built-in commission.

So Citadel accepted the commissions, and then simply credited their clients with the relevant amounts.

"People in the industry were really angry with us," recalls Wikus Marais. "Not only were we overturning the traditional way of doing business, but we were committing the cardinal sin of disclosing commissions to clients."

This wasn't the willful action of a maverick organisation. This was purely a question of establishing priorities.

The **road ahead** would be determined by the **power** of **relationships**, not transactions

From that very first line on that sheet of paper in that bachelor flat in Pretoria, Citadel knew that the road ahead would be determined by the power of relationships, not transactions.

There is a theory that says that a business that wants to become a market leader has to choose from one of three basic models of value. Operational efficiency, product leadership, or client intimacy. Citadel chose the latter.

"Looking back today," says Louis Fourie, "I really believe the decision to become a 'client intimate' business, offering investment advice, and not an investment business offering financial planning or investment products, helped us tremendously to create a huge barrier to entry in our market.

"The rules of the 'intimacy' offering were related to long-term trust, objectivity, and simplifying and customising solutions. All attributes which were not only scarce in the financial services industry, but expensive to establish as well."

Somewhat to the initial surprise of the Marais brothers, the majority of clients proved only too eager to embrace the concept of payment for financial advice, perhaps on the understanding that when it comes to free advice, you generally get what you pay for.

The first 100 clients of Citadel were signed up within three months of the company being formed, despite the conspicuous absence of a track record or service infrastructure.

"All we could give them," says Fourie, "was the promise that it was all about to happen."

Of course, there was another, more material incentive: "To nurse new clients into the business, we credited their fee accounts with the commissions still being paid over to us by the investment houses where we placed their money. This relieved them from having to make any upfront cash payments for the service. They were offered an extended honeymoon during which we had to honour our promise."

It was all part of the gameplan, which was unashamedly driven by one aspect of conventional thinking that Citadel was happy to adopt. Sell, sell, sell.

"There is a very simple name for the process of converting a theoretical solution into a business," says Fourie. "It's called selling. Great inventions and ideas die a quiet death on a daily basis, purely because of the inability of the inventors to convert their designs into sales."

CITADEL

Road to tomorrow… unleashing the power to share dreams and change people's lives

With neither the resources nor the inclination to launch a high-profile marketing and PR campaign, Citadel sold its services on the strength of word-of-mouth, adding an extra element of credibility by feeding selected financial journalists with lively titbits of economic comment and market analysis.

But what exactly was the company selling? Policies? Annuities? Portfolios? No, says Fourie.

"We were selling a dream and an ideal. We were selling the power to change people's lives."

It was that kind of thinking – a soft approach to hard issues – that earned Citadel its early reputation as a company with a certain aura, a culture that set it apart from the more aggressive stance of the typical private asset management house. The difference was one of structure as much as philosophy. For Citadel is an organisation of its time: Citadel is a business built on fractals.

Picture a particle of coloured light generated by mathematical equation, creating shifting, mesmerising patterns

Fourie... inside the fractal organisation

in a universe of chaos. Picture the fractal organisation: flexible, adaptable, driven by risk, averse to the rules of hierarchy, convention, and standard procedure. An organisation that revolves not around the needs of the corporation, but around the primary component of every successful enterprise. The individual.

"From the start," says Fourie, "we realised we needed to draw people who are more than intelligent, experienced or efficient.

"They must be people who project trust and sincerity, and live up to the demands inherent to a long-term relationship. People with depth of character."

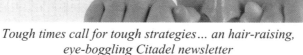

Tough times call for tough strategies… an hair-raising,
eye-boggling Citadel newsletter

Having enshrined the rejection of commission-based selling as its founding principle, Citadel began employing people – initially, old schoolmates, friends, former colleagues, even relatives – who could into fit either of two moulds, broadly defined as the Hunter or the Farmer.

The Hunter would concentrate on seeking and building new business, while the Farmer would uphold and maintain the professional relationship with the client on a daily basis. Today, these archetypes have evolved into Wealth Planners – responsible for structuring the portfolios of new investors – and Wealth Managers, who are responsible for giving ongoing advice and aftercare.

"The decision to create separate purposes for separate people," says Fourie, "has been a demanding one from a cash flow point of view, because of the initial lack of critical mass. We kicked off by paying Wealth Planners and Managers straight salaries based on a consensus view of their market value.

"This meant we had to finance the payroll from the income we generated by doing new business, and by attracting working capital."

It sounds like the standard bottom-line formula for any start-up business. But it doesn't necessarily apply in the field of financial services.

"It may sound silly," says Fourie, "but even today, virtually all of the established players steer away from serving both these goals. They either go for the 'sales at all cost' culture of the insurance industry, or they prefer the 'maintenance route' of the old private banking and stockbroking firms, without actively pursuing new business."

Which explains, in part, the continuing success of Citadel. A different structure, based on a different philosophy, revolving around a different set of individuals.

The founding brothers, along with Louis Fourie and the "Hunters and Farmers" who joined the company in the first two years, were, by nature, corporate defectors: people who didn't enjoy operating under a system of rigid rules and policies, in an environment defined by central control or autocratic supervision.

"We virtually took an oath," says Wikus Marais, "never to allow human talent or business spirit to be eroded by a prescriptive manual and company politics.

"We wanted to design a set of values and instil a culture that people would subscribe to of their own free will, because they believed in themselves, and they believed in the value the company offers."

It's a philosophy that extends well beyond the Hunters and Farmers at the core of Citadel's business, to encompass everyone who has a role to play in what Fourie calls "The Citadel Ecosystem".

He tells a tale of a "young Citadelion" named Pierre van Wyk, who approached him with the idea of involving the company's frontline staff – receptionists, drivers, tea ladies – in an ongoing campaign to "excite the client".

Impressed with Van Wyk's energy and enthusiasm, Fourie gave him a go-ahead and a budget, which was swiftly divided into weekly allowances for the frontline staff. No approvals or vouchers were required: all they had to do was spend the money on "adding value" to the business in their own unique way.

The effect on clients was immediate. Small, personalised touches, as simple as fresh flower blossoms placed on tea-trays, conveyed the aura of a company with an eye for detail, and a natural flair for connecting with the customer, in heart, in mind, in soul.

Quarsingh... a face of Citadel

Another example: when receptionist Judica Quarsingh encountered an unhappy client coming out of a meeting, she listened to his story and gave him two movie tickets for that evening, bought with her own weekly allowance. "Don't make any decisions until you've seen this movie!" she told him. The client was overwhelmed by her attitude, and is still a client today.

The programme, known internally as "The Face", has become an integral part of Citadel's relationship with its clients.

So many corporations speak glibly of "consumer connectedness" as a mainstay of their products, brands, or services; not many are able to put the philosophy into practise, at least beyond their warm-and-fuzzy marketing campaigns.

Citadel's head of Portfolio Management, Anton Musgrave, uses the familiar example of the Service Quality Questionnaire, which customers are invited to "take a few minutes to complete" in the understanding that this will help highlight and eliminate service-related shortcomings in an organisation.

Musgrave… inside the Thinkubator

For Citadel, such approaches are outdated and counterproductive.

"Why not just speak to clients one on one?" asks Musgrave. Which is precisely what Citadel takes pride in doing, in the form of regular "Thinkubator" sessions between clients and Citadelions. They're informal forums for sharing ideas, discussing new developments, debating trends in the marketplace.

"Clients love being involved in the success of a business," says Musgrave. "They like to know that they've got a role to play beyond the conventional boundaries of the client-business relationship. We also share our strategic inputs with our customers – they need to understand the context in which we do business. Every three months we have formal events around the country in which we take more than 3 000 clients and their families on a journey of discovery through changes in the world economy, new technologies and the implications for business and individuals. They love it. They value the way we continually challenge their thinking."

Citadel places little stock on titles and rigidly-defined positions, preferring the flexibility of the "flock of birds" model. Anyone can be part of the leadership process.

As Musgrave explains: "It's about putting the right people in the rights roles at the right times. This has lead to changes almost unthinkable in traditional corporate structures, such as when our then CEO was asked to take a small back office for a few months to write an urgently-needed new piece of

software. He just happened to be the best person for the role at that time, which meant someone else had to temporarily take over the role of CEO."

Finding and retaining the right people is a challenge for any company, particularly in a field as competitive as financial services. How does Citadel manage to get it right? Partly, says Musgrave, the answer lies in a corporate culture that gives staffers the same kind of focus and flexibility as they give their clients, while placing equal emphasis on the "unsung heroes" of the workforce.

"Citadelions are encouraged not to come to work on their spouse or children's birthdays," says Musgrave. "This is free time off, without leave forms. As a company, we recognise the natural desire each of us has to spend time with special people on special occasions. But it's more than just the time off.

It's the very spirit
and the core of a philosophy
built on the power of relationships.

If we want our staff to value client relationships highly, then we must treat our staff's relationships with their family and friends in the same way."

So what, then, is it going to be? A tax-effective annuity? An offshore portfolio? A hand-picked selection of equities, gilts and Government bonds? When all is said and done, it doesn't really matter.

The only free advice you need is this: it's never too late to plan your future.

All you need is a blank sheet of paper.

MY BLANK SLATE

Lessons Learnt

Understand the value of the value you add

Value can't be dressed up as hype,
or wrapped up in short-term greed

Great ideas die a quiet death, often because
innovators can't convert designs into sales

The creator of a new idea will not necessarily be
the ideal implementer

Success is determined by the power of relationships,
not transactions

Draw in people who project trust and sincerity, people with depth
of character

Sell a dream and an ideal, sell the power to change people's lives

Clients love being involved in the success of your business

Never underestimate the need for consistent, open and honest
communication, internally and externally

Don't let your beliefs be swayed by traditionalists, sceptics or
existing industry practices

Let the best individual at the time lead the 'flock of birds'

Plan your future on a blank sheet of paper

7

Flighting the Phoenix

Snatching innovation from the jaws of a downturn

How McCarthy Retail's Call-a-Car is adding new value propositions and profit streams in a commoditised industry

On a bright Monday morning in March, 2000, a young Cape Town journalist named Chris Botha arrives at a house in the smart Johannesburg suburb of Bryanston. Four bedrooms, pool, tennis court, expansive gardens. Botha looks around. For the next 90 days, this will be his home. More than that, it will be his world.

He will not be permitted to set foot outside the grounds, or drive beyond the high security gates. Wherever he wanders, he will be watched around the clock by nine strategically-positioned cameras. The house will be empty, devoid of all but the most basic conveniences and facilities.

But Botha will have access to one item that could help him endure the coming ordeal.

A computer with a high-speed connection to the Internet.

Botha grabs his belongings. Towel, mattress, sleeping-bag, pillow, bar of soap, toilet-roll. He walks up the stairs, accompanied by his sole authorised concession to the human need for companionship. A brindle bulldog named Henry.

Thus begins the Dotcoza Experiment, conducted by the firm of Andersen Consulting (now Accenture), to determine the answer to one of the most perplexing challenges of the early 21st Century. Can man survive on e-commerce alone?

The idea is that Botha will have to source his every need for day-to-day living – food, clothes, furniture, utensils, toiletries, entertainment – through the online portals that proudly claim to stand at the vanguard of a vibrant New Economy. Convenience! Access! Security! Delivery! Here is the promise of a world where e stands for everything your heart desires.

The world of e-commerce, e-business, "e-tail", where merchants with minimal overheads compete to bring the goods directly from the warehouse to your door. Yes, as Botha will soon discover, it is entirely possible to sustain life at the click of a mouse. All you need, apart from the technology, is a valid credit-card number and an endless reservoir of patience.

But in retrospect, in the cold light of the dot.com downturn, perhaps the question needs to be rephrased. The issue is not whether you can survive on the Internet. The question is: why would you want to?

There is a world out there, a world of tangible products, face-to-face service, instant gratification and communal belonging. We are social animals. We need to connect, we need to interact. We need to see, touch, feel, taste, and smell the merchandise before we part with our cash. Sure, e-commerce is fine for books, DVD's, maybe the occasional bar of soap or can of dogfood.

But as Botha will observe, when his 90 days are up: "You still can't buy a motorcar online." Then again, you probably wouldn't want to. For all the convenience of life in a cocoon, clicking the tyres just isn't the same as kicking them. But wait.

What if you could have the best of both worlds?

Let's leave the house in Bryanston now, and take a quick at the real world.

McCarthy Retail. One of South Africa's largest retail conglomerates. At 86 years old, one of the oldest, too. Within McCarthy Retail, resides South Africa's premier motor retailer: McCarthy Motor Holdings.

Since 1997 McCarthy Retail has fallen on hard times. The retail market has shrunk and transformed almost beyond recognition. There is a prolonged recession in the furniture, clothing and building supplies businesses. The

turbulence affects the South African automotive market, and sales volumes and margins suffer.

McCarthy Retail goes through a **traumatic** period in 1998, posting an attributable loss of R328,9 million. The Group's furniture arm, Beares, which employs more than 9 600 people, creates a R1,4 billion debt problem.

The company is apparently spinning out of control. Its share price is dwindling.

In this difficult environment, one of South Africa's most respected businessmen, Brand Pretorius, joins the McCarthy board. Previously managing director of Toyota SA Marketing – during his tenure, the company became South Africa's largest vehicle manufacturer – this former South African Marketing Person of the Year takes over the mantle of McCarthy Motor Holdings.

With nine franchises and over 115 dealerships, McCarthy Motor Holdings is South Africa's biggest seller of new and used cars. But in the mid-90's, that was a distinction that wasn't necessarily good for business. In 1995, as part of its trade liberalisation policy, the Government introduced a scheme known as MIDP: the Motor Industry Development Plan.

Pretorius... riding the storm

Import duties on new vehicles would be lowered, and manufacturers would be encouraged to produce for export. The impact on pricing and competition was immediate. But as the customer reaped the benefits, the industry was thrown into chaos. Suddenly, you could buy a brand-new Toyota for less than the cost of a comparable second-hand vehicle.

McCarthy, with its large national network of used-car dealers, was particularly hard-hit.

"In real terms," says Pretorius, "some of our franchises were selling used cars at below cost price. Margins were falling, losses were mounting. At the same time new vehicle profitability started deteriorating as well, due to intense competition. Traditionally McCarthy Motor Holdings derived more than 50% of its profits from new vehicle trading activity. With the number of manufacturers and importers increasing from 7 to more than 20, new vehicle margins also plummeted. We urgently had to come up with a strategy to reverse these trends."

Lourens Botha: "U-commerce is the future of business."

Pretorius has a fundamental view of retailing:

"Today, **competition** is no longer between products, competition is between **business models**".

So clearly there was a need to capitalise on new business models to create future growth and new markets. The Internet was available as a platform for doing business electronically.

But how to find the capital injection to explore these new opportunities in a corporation so strapped for cash? How do you capitalise on the opportunities of the digital age without breaking the bank?

Answer: you get radical! You find a young, innovative entrepenurial thinker who is not afraid to experiment and take risks.

Enter Lourens Botha, no relation to the Dotcoza guy. Then a strategic planning executive at McCarthy, Botha fully understands the constraints the business is under. His big strength lies in his ability to harness his network of relationships and commercialise new ideas quickly, and at low cost. His special field of expertise: e-commerce, e-business, e-tail. But forget the e for a moment.

As Botha explains, the real key to winning and holding the customer can be found a little further down the alphabet. The real key is U.

"**U-commerce**," says Lourens Botha, "is the way things are moving. U-commerce is the **future of business**."

The U stands for Universal. Universal channels, universal possibilities. It could be a customer strolling from the street into your showroom. It could be a customer scrolling through a web-page late at night. It could be the beep of an SMS on a cellphone, inviting a customer to attend a special preview sale. It could be a call to a call centre, or an ad on interactive television. It's everything at once, everything in harmony. It's business, the way U want it.

Gone is the notion of Real vs. Virtual, Bricks vs. Clicks. The new mantra is **integration**. It's a word Lourens Botha uses a lot.

As the managing director of McCarthy Online, the Internet division of McCarthy Retail, Botha's job – his calling, his obsession – is to break new ground and explore new horizons for a group that has always been rooted in

the kind of goods you need to try before you buy. Furniture, clothing, footwear, building supplies. And more than anything else, motor vehicles.

Botha had a feeling that the answer might lie in a brand-new vehicle. Not another Toyota or Mercedes; a new vehicle for driving the business.

As it happened, there was a **nearly-new model,** low mileage, mechanically-sound, **road-tested** with flying colours in **the toughest** auto market in the world. It was a model called CarMax, and Botha came across it on a field trip to the USA in 1995. Owned by Circuit City, a chain of electronic and computer retailers, CarMax was a network of used-car superstores, driven by a straightforward business proposition: buying a car shouldn't have to be a nightmare.

You shouldn't have to **trek** from town to town, lot to lot, just to find a vehicle **to suit your** needs. You shouldn't have to **haggle,** you shouldn't have to **hassle.** But on top of that, the real deal was technology. You could arrive at your dealer of choice, fully informed, fully prepared, ready to do business.

Could this be the strategy McCarthy was looking for? A superstore, offering a wide selection of quality-tested vehicles, backed by computer databases and slick, user-friendly technologies that would finally catapult used-car buying into the digital age. Back home, Botha wasted no time getting his vision into gear.

It would start in Gauteng, with a huge store alongside the M1 freeway, in full view of the passing traffic. Whether you used the off-ramp, the telephone, or the Internet, this would be the place to come to buy a good-as-new used car. A site was identified, artist's impressions were commissioned, **financial models** were drawn up.

In mid-1996, only a few months after this trip to the States, Botha presented his proposal to the board of McCarthy Motor Holdings. There was much interest, much nodding of heads, much juggling of spreadsheets and calculators.

The board gave its answer: No.

There was nothing inherently wrong with the concept, aside from its timing: the market was still too depressed, the venture too risky, unproven,

Build a **bigger** store,
the biggest in the country,
a store **so big** that it could only exist
in a **place without walls,**
borders, or **boundaries**
...a place like the Internet

and expensive. On top of that, McCarthy Retail had limited financial capacity due to the strain put on its resources by its non-motor interests.

Back at the drawing-board, Botha mulled the proposal over with Brand Pretorius.

The easy, obvious route would have been to abandon the CarMax idea altogether. After all, McCarthy already owned and ran dozens of used-car dealerships across the country. Why build another, bigger, geographically-limited store, when…wait. That was it!

Don't build a big store next to the highway. Build a bigger store, the biggest in the country, a store so big that it could only exist in a place without walls, borders, or boundaries...a place like the Internet.

You would be able to go shopping for your car, narrow down your choice and take your selected vehicle for a "spin" without leaving your home. You'd be able to search for a car in your own time, at your own pace, drilling down through models, types, years, price-ranges and locations, until you came up with a shortlist of likely contenders. The concept would also allow McCarthy Motor Holdings to break free from its geographical boundaries and sell nationally, not only in those areas where it had dealerships.

In October, 1996, Botha approaches Pretorius with a revised strategic proposal. Create a "virtual" used-car superstore, capable of hosting McCarthy's **entire inventory** on the Internet. Link it to a call centre, manned around the clock, with agents who will respond promptly to queries and arrange test-drives at the customer's nearest McCarthy dealership.

Make it, from the start, a dual-medium initiative: if you don't have access to the Internet, dial the call centre and let an agent guide you through the process on the phone. Call it e-commerce, call it teleshopping, but whatever you call it…call it Call-a-Car.

This time, when the proposal is presented to the McCarthy board, the answer isn't "No"; it's "Well, yes, but..." Much of the scepticism still revolves around the delicate question of spending money on an untried concept in a depressed economy.

In retrospect, R10 million doesn't sound like much of an outlay for the launch of a Blue Chip Internet startup, especially when you break it down to a monthly operating budget of R2 800 for each of the 100 dealerships then in the McCarthy stable. But this was 1997, and McCarthy Call-a-Car was a sales and marketing vehicle with no visible warranty attached.

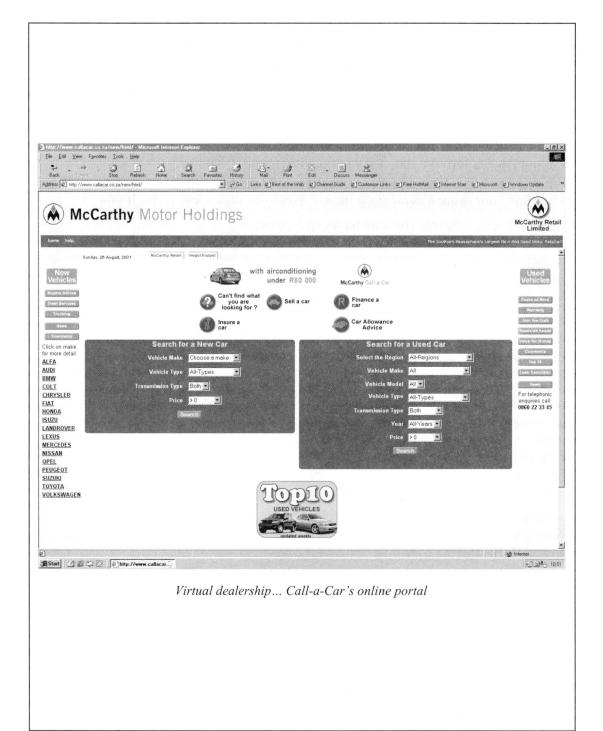

Virtual dealership… Call-a-Car's online portal

What if it turned out to be all flash and no substance? What if consumers just saw it as a gimmick? What if dealers saw it as a threat to their walk-in trade? What if the whole system came crashing down whenever anyone tried to use it? There was only one way to find out.

At the end of August, 1997, after months of planning and testing, McCarthy Call-a-Car goes live. Over 3 000 vehicles stand ready for browsing, at , or through the direct call-centre number. The way it works is simple. You make your choice, you leave your details online or on the phone, and your nearest dealer gets back to you to arrange a test-drive. If you like, they'll even bring the car to your door.

"Initially," recalls Botha, "people just thought it was too good to be true. We had to convince them that the system actually worked."

For the dealers in the group, compelled to make monthly contributions to the marketing and maintenance of the site, Call-a-Car was positioned as the ultimate lead-generating mechanism. All you had to do was sit back and wait for the business, from customers who would already have a good idea of the stock you had on your lot.

Trouble was, many dealers also thought it was too good to be true. Calls weren't returned, customers were left stranded, crank-callers and other time-wasters clogged up the system. But Botha knew that the model was sound. All it would take was a little education, experience, and word-of-mouth on both sides of the equation. This wasn't a dot.com hype. This was the real deal.

"We didn't set out to reinvent the wheel," says Botha. "We just put a bit of a spin on it. We placed a new way of doing business on top of an existing dealership infrastructure. All we wanted to do was take the grudge and hassle out of a buying a vehicle."

Backed by a hard-hitting, "no budget" Press and TV campaign – two commercials were shot for R25 000 in a used-car lot on a Sunday morning – Call-a-Car slowly started generating real interest, real leads, real sales. From an average of 50 vehicles a month in late-1997, the figure jumped to 102 sold in September, 1998, and 403 a year later. No doubt about it. Call-a-Car was getting business on the road.

But these were the worst of times for McCarthy Retail. In October 1999, Pretorius was appointed CEO of the McCarthy Retail Group. "So many

The mouse that roared... slick advertising drove the success of the Call-a-Car concept

things went wrong for us that year," he recalls. "The Beares debtors book debacle, the Asian economic crisis, the inability to list McCarthy Motor Holdings because of market conditions, a collapse in business confidence and soaring interest rates.

"That we got through it all shows the resilience of the group. The Call-a-Car success was one of the few highlights of that year."

By 2001, Call-a-Car could boast annual sales of close on 6 000 vehicles, and net profit of more than R10 million. McCarthy's share of the used-car market had risen from under 10 per cent in 1995, to just under 12 per cent. New vehicles, added to the mix in early 2001, were making up 15 per cent of sales. Because of the incremental sales generated through Call-a-Car, McCarthy Motor Holdings achieved record profits for the financial year ended June 2001. Due to much reduced reliance on new vehicle profitability, the group's business model is now far more robust than ever before.

But for Lourens Botha, the real vindication lies beyond the bottom line, in the clear-cut proof that the Internet is a viable medium for setting-up and sealing a deal. More than 40 percent of Call-a-Car's business is currently generated on the Web, as opposed to 5 per cent in 1997. Closing ratios for Web-based enquiries are also higher than they are for telephonic callers.

It's easy to see why. The Web customer is likely to spend more time searching and researching, more time filtering and narrowing-down the choice. The Web customer, says Botha, will be more aware, more informed, more demanding. The big challenge for business today is to be able to meet that demand, and to remember that it doesn't begin and end with the click of a mouse.

Ubiquitous, unbounded, universal, u-commerce allows the retailer to capture the customer in traditional and digital ways, and sets up the very real prospect of keeping that customer for life. But it's more than just a question of storing and manipulating information on a database. The real key, says Botha, is

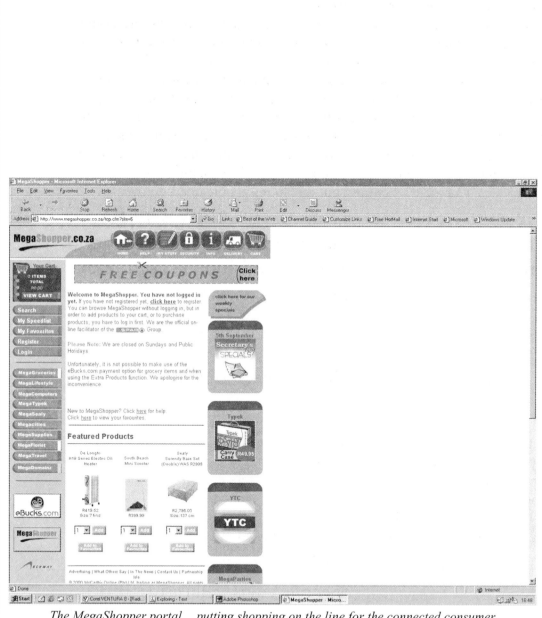

The MegaShopper portal… putting shopping on the line for the connected consumer

adding value, and adding value means subtracting as much of the hassle and risk as you can from every transaction.

Of course, it pays to remember, in today's everywhere-at-once marketplace, that not every transaction is going to be viewed in the same light by the customer. The boutique shopper, for instance, will relish the prospect of spending an hour or so in an upmarket delicatessen, smelling, eyeing, and maybe even tasting the tempting range of goods on display.

The grocery shopper, on the other hand, will usually just want to fill a trolley with the essentials on a list, and get down to the tiresome business of unpacking the bags as swiftly as possible. For Botha, this is where the big opportunity lies. Don't try to compete with shopping as a sensory experience. Compete by cutting out the things people don't enjoy.

With this philosophy in mind, **McCarthy Online** has **grown** beyond the new and used vehicles on Call-a-Car, to **encompass** everything from **canned food** to **computers** on a Web portal called **MegaShopper.** While the market is small – just over 1 000 regular shoppers – the venture was able to break even within 18 months, and a deal with the Spar chain has given it access to one of the country's largest retail networks.

The point is, **online retailing** does work, but it **doesn't work in a vacuum.** It needs the impetus of big, recognisable, trustworthy brands, and it needs the combination of high-tech and high-touch that has helped to make Call-a-Car such a success. And when the South Africa car market began to take off again in January 2001, Call-a-Car was in place to ride the new wave of consumers coming into the market. International recognition for the Call-a-Car concept came in July 2001, when it was applauded by the Automotive Fellowship International as an outstanding and unique example of real innovation in motor retailing.

The development and implementation of innovative concepts needs patience, time, and – more than anything else – the backing of restless, radical thinkers who won't take no for an answer.

Pretorius' words continue to resonate through the business: "Competition is no longer between products, competition is between business models"

"In any large organisation," says Botha, "you will get custodians of the status quo, who frown on new ideas that initially seem a bit crazy and appear to cost a lot of money. You need courage and perseverance to continue. You need newcomers to break the mould and make things happen."

It also helps, of course, to have the support of top management, in this case Brand Pretorius, who was prepared to invest in innovation, even at the worst of times.

True, in an age of spectacular crashes and dot.com disasters, there is something to be said for a certain healthy scepticism in the face of any new business proposal that is prefixed by an e, an i, or even a u. But the point is, there's no escaping the future.

"Perhaps the most profound lesson of all," says Botha, "is that technology is changing the shape of business. It is educating customers and making them a lot more aware and demanding. The customer of the future is digitally-orientated by nature, and will use multiple digital devices to shop and do business. If you're not ready to deal with them, prepare to go out of business."

At the higher level, the story of McCarthy Retail's difficulties is by no means over. In August 2001, a bold plan was put in place for the financial restructuring of the debt-ridden group. The plan involves a R1,1 billion capital injection to put McCarthy on a sound financial footing and enable it to return to its core business of motor retailing.

"Reshaping McCarthy Retail is the biggest challenge I have faced," says Pretorius, "but it has not been an intimidating one. Apart from driving strategy for the group in the years ahead, my function must be to create demand. We have to be continually innovative. If we don't have customers, we don't have a business."

Pretorius... continually innovative

This innovative thinking is likely to continue to have profound impact at McCarthy Retail, as the Group sets out to give flight to its own corporate Phoenix.

MY ACTION PLANS

Lessons Learnt

There's no escaping the future

Technology is changing the shape of business

Capitalise on innovations of others

Today, competition is no longer between products,
it's between business models

Every opportunity is perishable

Irrelevancy is a bigger risk than inefficiency

8

The Tail Wagging the Dog

Taking on the world's biggest players from a garage

How Mark Shuttleworth sold his business, demonstrating the epitome of perfect timing

At the edge of the known universe, at the point on the map where knowledge and understanding give way to fear, conjecture and speculation, the mapmakers of old would inscribe a warning to those foolhardy enough to venture into uncharted territories.

"Hic sunt dracones," it would read. Here be dragons. Fire-breathing monsters with leathery wings, gaping jaws, and flesh-tearing talons, they would lie in wait for ships that sailed too far and plunged off the end of the world, sending their crews screaming into the bottomless abyss. Today, of course, we know better.

There are no dragons. The world is round. All you need to navigate it is an up-to-date map, an eye for the distant horison, and a vessel custom-built to transport your dreams to the shores of glorious reality. And yet, as Korzybski wrote in *Science and Sanity* in 1941, the map is not the territory.

Sometimes, even when you think you know where you are going, fate and the winds of change have a way of steering your ship on a very different course, usually at the very last minute.

Take Mark Shuttleworth, for example.

In 1995, he is a final-year student of Business Science at the University of Cape Town. Like many of his fellow students, he is an unashamed "party animal", enjoying an active social life on and off the campus. But unlike many, he has shied away from lining up a job for his first year in the real world, pinning his hopes instead on a scholarship that will allow him to devote his energies to the relative languor of post-graduate study.

Shuttleworth... chasing dragons

It is not as if Shuttleworth, then only 21, is opposed to the notion of a hard day's work in return for a living wage. On the contrary, he has carved himself a lucrative niche as a freelance consultant to companies seeking to know more about a fledgling force for information, communication, and – who knows? – maybe even commerce. The Internet.

So enthused and intrigued is Shuttleworth by the money-making possibilities of the medium, that he spends as many hours online as he does in argument with those faculty members who dispute his notion that the Internet has a role to play in the realm of Business Science.

It is, as he is frequently reminded, little more than a forum for inter-varsity communication, secondary research, and mindless diversion, summed up by the unproductive, time-obliterating pursuit known as "surfing the Web". But all this becomes academic on the day Shuttleworth learns he has failed in his bid to secure a post-graduate scholarship.

For the straight-A student, it is a blow to the ego that leaves him reeling. With nothing but burning ambition and a Bachelor of Business Science degree to his credit, he falls back on Plan B, forming a small consulting company whose very name suggests a radically different way of thinking.

Thawte.

Operating from the garage of his parents' home
in Durbanville, Cape Town,
typically attired in shorts, sandals, and tee-shirt,
Shuttleworth boldly sets sail for the jaws of waiting dragons.

His chosen terrain, borderless and seemingly boundless, is the terra incognita of the Internet, where vast fortunes may be reaped by those who can conquer the credit-card bandits, the identity-thieves, the hackers and pirates of the high seas of electronic commerce.

The weapon for good in this war is a piece of binary code called a digital certificate, which acts as a passport or ID document for anyone seeking peace of mind in their dealings with online merchants. Through a protocol called SSL (Secure Sockets Layer), credit-card numbers and other electronic data are scrambled and encrypted before transmission, allowing for easy authentication and rock-solid security of transaction.

Since fear of fraud has always been the single biggest obstacle to the growth of online commerce, digital certificates have become the most sought-after seals of approval and warrants of passage of the new age of business.

And it is here that Mark Shuttleworth, CEO and sole employee of Thawte Consulting, sets out to build a humble little business for himself.

Well, not so humble, and not so little. By the turn of the millennium – only four years after his graduation from UCT – Shuttleworth will have sold his company to his biggest rival, the American giant VeriSign, for US$575 million, or R3,5 billion. Famously, Shuttleworth will reward all 60 employees of Thawte (including two cleaners and a gardener) with R1 million each. Some will become part of VeriSign; some will join Shuttleworth in setting up a bold new business venture.

Grandly headquartered in Cape Town, the new company will manage assets and provide venture capital for fledgling entrepreneurs with big dreams and feasible ideas. The company will be called HBD. Which stands for: Here be Dragons.

The chief dragon-chaser himself will shift his base to London, running HBD and an education-oriented philanthropic foundation, TSF (The Shuttleworth Foundation), in-between training to be the second civilian in space at Star City in Moscow. Yes, there are new territories to be conquered, on earth and among the stars.

But the big question remains: how did Shuttleworth do it? He answers with a shrug and an impish smile.

Mark Shuttleworth and the HBD team... beyond Thawte

"The usual suspects.
Luck, timing, foolhardy bravery
in the face of insurmountable odds,
inspiration, perspiration, blood, sweat, and tears."

Certainly, it is impossible to find fault with Shuttleworth's sense of timing. His deal with VeriSign went through just a few months before the company shed billions from its market value, as one of many victims of the meltdown in the global IT industry. As for luck, Shuttleworth has always been prepared to take the bad along with the good. What if he had won his post-graduate scholarship? What if he had lined up a steady, secure job with a large corporation?

"If life were totally predictable," he says, "it would be far less enjoyable.
The temptation for a lot of success-driven people is to be miserable if they don't get what they want in every situation. I fight hard to get what I want – ask the people who have to work with me – but when things don't work out that way I accept there's a reason, and I start looking for the silver lining or the new opportunity."

But in the end, as Shuttleworth is quick to attest, it all comes down to three things. Blood, sweat, tears. With its vast resources and huge customer base in the US, VeriSign may have appeared to exist in a realm beyond open challenge, particularly from a backyard operator at the opposite end of the planet.

But in a sphere of business where superiority of geographic location soon becomes irrelevant, Shuttleworth pushed the boundaries, and nudged the giant, through a combination of aggressive pricing and a focus on such lesser-served markets as Australia and Europe.

More than that, Shuttleworth outsmarted VeriSign and his other competitors with his innovative approach to digital certification, issuing single, encrypted certificates that allowed a company to register and certify all of its customers and employees at once.

The strategy paid off, over and over again. By 2000, Thawte owned 40 percent of the global digital certification market, and was generating revenue of US$90 000 a month, at prices that were two-thirds lower than

VeriSign's. That's when the tail began wagging the dog. That's when VeriSign began making manoeuvres.

Still, Shuttleworth will be the first to admit that he still sometimes has second thoughts about Thawte.

"We could have been more aggressive in marketing some of our more industry-changing products," he says, citing cross-certification of companies as an example.

"We could have worked harder to sign up large ISP's as customers. And we could have created a higher priced product to compete at the high end of the market. I still don't understand pricing psychology. But the trick is to be happy with the way things work out, irrespective of the outcome."

More important than **acknowledging** your **mistakes**, says Shuttleworth, is **learning not to lose sleep** over them.

It's all part of a business and personal philosophy that puts passion ahead of all other criteria for running with a project.

"Above all," he advises, "find a project you can be truly passionate about. That might mean refusing projects that have better financial prospects, or are more mainstream, or have less overt risk. The big mistake is to try to find the 'Next Big Thing' based on what others are saying. By the time people are talking about it you are probably too far behind... you need to find the thing that resonates with yourself and your interests and your skills. And you need to build a strategy for success with the pieces you have at your disposal rather than the pieces you would like to have.

"Also, know what's **really** important to you, and **make sure** that you **always stay true** to that. The temptation to sacrifice everything to the pursuit of money or recognition is enormous and gets stronger the more successful you become. Remember that nobody ever died wishing they'd spent more time at the office. I'm always at the office, but then I'm also always in the playground. That's what's important to me."

What is also important to remember is that Shuttleworth pursued his own passion, and started his own enterprise, without the customary security of a large corporate sponsor or a tidy sum of venture capital. Looking back, he believes that the lack of venture funding was a negative that became a

*Shuttleworth... turning lack of venture capital from a
negative into a positive*

positive, inspiring him to work harder, faster, and smarter in a fiercely competitive market.

But now that he is in a position to distribute venture capital himself, what are the qualities he looks for in other dragon-chasers with other passions to pursue? He counts off the checklist.

"Insight into how the world is evolving. An understanding of what is important and what is irrelevant. A willingness to take the difficult path rather than the easy one if it means a better long term position. Recognition of the fact that money can create as many problems for a start-up as it can solve. Clear insight into the fundamental forces at work within the marketplace. A plan to generate cash from operations, even if indirectly. And finally, a willingness to convince friends with high paying steady jobs and good career prospects to join the venture *before* it raises finance!"

Today, having swapped his shorts, sandals and tee-shirt for casual slacks, golf shirts, and sensible shoes, Shuttleworth is upheld as a role-model of innovative entrepreneurship in action, even if he has faced criticism for relocating to London and indulging his boyhood fantasy of soaring into the cosmos.

But he shrugs off any tributes to his business acumen, insisting that he could use "a lot more discipline and training…for better or worse I've never been part of a large organisation, and it shows."

Still, when it comes to confronting dragons, he is clearly a man who is able to overcome his own worst fears. Which doesn't mean he has an inordinate appetite for risk.

"I'm actually pretty risk averse by nature," he says. "I try to understand as many of the parameters as possible before taking a decision, which can make for painfully slow decision making and decisions that get reversed...sometimes repeatedly. I'm not very easy to work with.

"But the one thing I am totally fearless about is peer pressure. I'm absolutely willing to do something even if everybody else thinks its a bad idea, if I'm confident that I have thought it through and can see a strategy for success. The strategy may fail, but if I think it's worth a shot I'll not ask permission or for anybody else's blessing.

Half the fun is trying things that other people won't try.
That doesn't mean jumping off a cliff
to see what happens.

It means being open to ideas that other people are not open to, simply because of their worldview."

From backyard garage to top of the world,
from Cape Town to London to Outer Space,
Mark Shuttleworth has managed to grasp
the starry heights that others can only dream of.

But how, when you are not yet 30 and you are rich enough to spend US$20 million on a ride into space, do you manage to retain the hunger that drove you to succeed and innovate in the first place?

"It's too early to say what I'm capable of doing in the future," says Shuttleworth. "I do find it much more difficult to pursue new ideas now, because I have so much less time to play with the Lego, so to speak. And so many more options...trying to find the space in which to focus is tough.

"What I'm trying to do is filter out all the things that are less interesting in favour of the ideas that genuinely pique my curiosity. The other thing I'm trying very hard to do is refuse to live inside the box other people create for me. In the eyes of many people I'm a 'business guy'.

"I'm not really. Nor am I a programmer, or a philanthropist, a technologist or even a networking guy. I'm me. All of those things, none of them, and some other pieces too. A whole mix of interests and ideas. And I hope to pursue each of those ideas, one by one, till my time is up.

"The result could be a complete mess,
or a symphony,
but at least it will be my mess."

INNOVATION OPPORTUNITIES

Lessons Learnt

Find a project you can be truly passionate about

Relish the bad luck as much as the good

Don't lose sleep over your mistakes

Don't be afraid to try things other people won't try

The Next Big Thing is always
something no-one is yet talking about

Timing is everything

Once you've made it,
find the courage to be yourself and have some fun

9

Harvesting ideas

The process of finding and funding radical innovation

How Deloitte Touche Tohmatsu's global approach to harvesting ideas and fuelling innovation was born out of South Africa

Think. Think in the shower, think in the traffic, think when you're spinning up a hill on your cycle in the gym. Think when your mind is empty, think when it's weighed down with worry. Think, because that's the way the world turns: on the axis of an idea whose time has come. Let's see.

How about a flavoured utensil, such as a wooden spoon, that automatically soaks your food in garlic or oregano oil as you stir it on the stove. How about a toothbrush that automatically fills up with toothpaste when you press a button on the handle. How about beer that glows in the dark.

How about a pill with a time-released coating of caffeine, that automatically flows through your veins and wakes you after a hard and heavy night. How about a daily newspaper called *Lunch*, that is wrapped around your breadroll or burger to give you something to read while you're eating it. Sounds crazy, right? Of course.

We're at HalfBakery.Com, an online forum for the sharing and airing of ideas that are wild or outrageous or – every now and again – so sensible and practical that you wonder why nobody thought of them before.

The point is, somebody probably has, just as somebody once thought of trapping electricity in the filaments of a glass bulb, or squeezing waves of

**Deloitte
Touche
Tohmatsu**

About Us

Services

Industries

Locations

Careers

Publications

What's New

Site Search

Feedback

Wherever you are in the world, we'll make your business count.

The national practices of Deloitte Touche Tohmatsu are dedicated to delivering world-class service to our world-class clients in more than 130 countries.

Our mission is to help our clients and our people excel. These two forces come together in a powerful combination of wide-ranging services in every major business center in the world.

Our services include assurance and advisory, management consulting, and tax advice to hundreds of the world's biggest and most respected companies, including the world's largest manufacturer, 5 of the 25 largest banks and four of the largest trading companies.

Our people also listen in over 100 languages; beyond the major economies many of our professionals serve and assist the emerging markets, advising governments and institutions throughout Central Europe and Asia Pacific.

Globalization, changing societal priorities, and access to real-time information are fundamentally changing the way organizations do business. We help our clients meet the challenge of demonstrating globally responsible business practices while balancing social, environmental, and financial performance.

To find out more about what Deloitte Touche Tohmatsu can do for you, explore our Web site.

**Which Big Five Firm is running
rings around its competition?**

the answer is
**Deloitte
Touche
Tohmatsu**

*Deloitte Touche Tohmatsu's online portal, gateway to a web of
services that encircle the world*

sound down a length of cable, or transmitting text and images through fine strands of fibre at 4 320 terabits a second.

Every idea, no matter how fanciful, no matter how lucid, begins as a chain of thought floating freely through the ether.

The challenge is to bring it down to earth, to tether it to a business plan and a venture capital budget, to release it into the wild and see how fast and how far it travels before it takes root.

Want to hear something really crazy? Okay.

Imagine you're in charge of the South African division of a business that is already the biggest in a big league, already Number One by any measure, be it Earnings Per Partner, Earnings Per Professional, Earnings Per Capita. Imagine it's 1996, and your revenue stream, based on historic growth patterns, is expected to reach, let's say, R950 million by the end of the next four years.

You already have plans to grow in excess of 20% per year. Imagine that's not enough for you. Pluck a figure from the air – make it R1,2 billion – instantly doubling your projected growth rate – and commit your company to reaching that goal, somehow, someway, within the same time-frame.

"Now that," says Louis Geeringh, double-dotting an i on a whiteboard for emphasis, "is innovation driven by a radical view of the future."

We're in the Johannesburg headquarters of Deloitte & Touche, the South African member firm of Deloitte Touche Tohmatsu, the global

Geeringh and fellow innovators

professional services firm that employs close to 100 000 people in 133 countries. Their client include more than 700 blue chip companies with turnovers in excess of US$1 billion each. Geeringh, though originally only having South African responsibilities for strategic business development, now has world-wide responsibilities and his official title is Global Executive

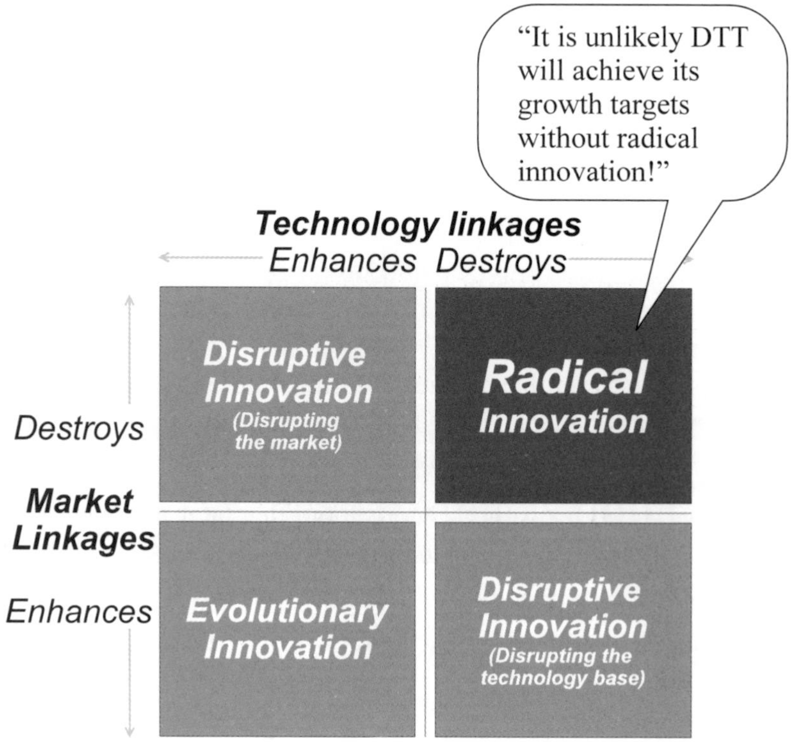
"It is unlikely DTT will achieve its growth targets without radical innovation!"
Technology linkages
Enhances
Destroys
Market Linkages
Destroys
Enhances
Disruptive Innovation (Disrupting the market)
Radical Innovation
Evolutionary Innovation
Disruptive Innovation (Disrupting the technology base)

Director of Service Innovation, which means…well, let's get back to the whiteboard and the South African part of the story.

"You see, in South Africa we wanted to radically grow the business, so we took an intellectual decision to benchmark and hit a target that wasn't backed up by the usual market research, and had no apparent foundation in our existing business. We committed ourselves to finding an extra R300 million in revenue, in an economy that grows by 2 per cent per annum."

Geeringh pauses, felt-tip in hand, taking a long, hard look at the rough graph of Time vs Revenue.

"In other words, we committed ourselves to creating something out of a void. We were determined to step into the risky world of radical innovation. Evolutionary change alone would not cut it."

The void, of course, is where all ideas are born, and here the idea was to build a place where ideas themselves could be incubated, nurtured, given shape and form. Not a building of bricks and mortar. Deloitte Touche Tohmatsu already has enough of those.

This would be a space rather than a place, a forum where fleeting thoughts could be herded, exposed to heat and light, and – assuming they passed the test – transformed into something approaching solid matter. Globally this would be... The Innovation Zone. More about that later in the story.

Which brings an immediate question to mind. What does innovation have to do with Deloitte Touche Tohmatsu? How can you realistically encourage a large successful established hierarchical business to become passionate about generating ideas and re-inventing itself? How can you possibly deliver on such a promise?

Their territory, after all, is primarily audit, accounting and tax consultancy. This is the firm started by William Welch Deloitte, the

Radical innovation is critical to achieving DTT's growth strategy

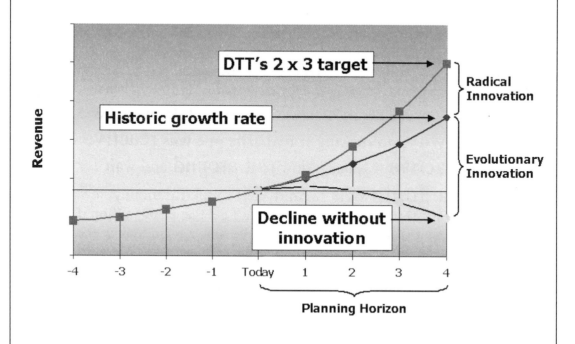

19th Century adventurer turned accountant, and George Touch, the Scottish auditor who added an e to the end of his name because he was tired of correcting Englishmen who didn't know that it was supposed to rhyme with "loch". The thing is, in the space of a hundred years, a lot more than a name can change.

Today, Deloitte Touche Tohmatsu – that's Admiral Nobuzo Tohmatsu, the Japanese naval attaché who became a public accountant at the age of 57, and went on to head up the firm that would eventually find a global partner big enough to match its own ambitions – is still in the tax and auditing business. But when you're that deep in a company's books, you begin to get a sense of the prospects and possibilities that lie beyond the bottom line.

So today, under the broad umbrella of "professional services", Deloitte & Touche in South Africa includes everything from legal services to recruitment to private banking to the management of knowledge and custom software development.

"We would not have fathomed," says Louis Geeringh, "that we would one day be employing lawyers, rocket scientists, and pizza-eating, pony-tailed people who lock themselves in a room and write code."

Which brings us back to innovation, and the small matter of the R300 million gap in South Africa where the story started. In 1996, when that spur-of-the-moment "intellectual decision" was taken, there were two possible pathways to making it real. The one was reactive; the other, proactive. Meaning: don't sit around and wait for the Big Idea. Jump right in, and start making money.

"We knew," says Geeringh, "that we wouldn't get that R300 million if we sat back and waited for things to happen. We took a good look at the business we were in, and more importantly, the businesses we weren't. There were some obvious opportunities. We weren't in financial services, we weren't in technology consulting, we weren't in human capital consulting.

"Those ideas, we could put directly into development. We went out and hired a bunch of people from very diverse backgrounds and competencies – corporate finance, economics and project management, but with a passion

Welcome to the zone... setting out to turn dreams into reality

for business building as a common denominator and doing without a manual. 'Guys,' we said, 'we need to make an extra R300 million over the next four years. Get out there, identify new business opportunities and formulate a plan how we can enter the market quickly and in a big way. We realised to achieve this, we would have to buy companies, integrate them, make them work.'"

Then there was the other option.
Look into the void. Adjust your eyes to the darkness. Switch on the light. And make something out of nothing.

The Deloitte Touche Tohmatsu Innovation Zone, it turns out, is the key to growing the business beyond its historical, scientifically backed-up projections, by allowing anyone who has a stake in that growth to participate in the free generation of new business ideas.

The Innovation Zone is a website, in the public domain, accessible to anyone with a 'deloitte' in their e-mail address. It's more than a think tank, more than a suggestion box. It's the bedrock of the future, and the future, as everyone knows, begins with the click of a mouse on a button marked SUBMIT.

Whatever your position in the organisation, wherever in the world you may be, you log-in, submit your proposal – a few lines, a few hundred words, the system helps you structure the outline of a business plan – and you sit back and wait for the gears to turn.

"Every idea goes into a database, and the interactive system forces it to fly through the internal processes, there's no logjam created by the hierarchy, " says Geeringh. "From there, it's judged according to a universal scoring system, on the basis of its overall feasibility and viability. If it fails, it stays on the database, because even the wildest of ideas might turn out to have merit or relevance further down the line. If it passes, it goes onto the next stage. The interview."

Here, an internal panel will quiz the progenitor or progenitors of the proposal, seeking to explore the deeper thinking behind it, and analyse any

A comprehensive approach to finding and funding innovation

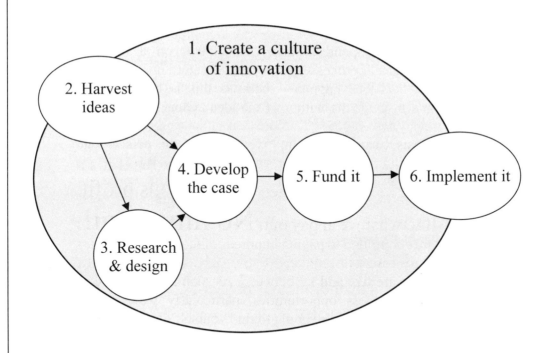

other ideas that have spun off or developed from the original free-floating thought. The next step: maturity.

The idea is championed, supported, protected from the "corporate antibodies" that rally by reflex against anything that looks too different or looks like it might cost too much money.

The idea, which has now become a matured value proposition, is then submitted to further scrutiny by an extended panel, made up of knowledgeable Deloitte staff as well as outside experts and possibly even clients. After this stage, says Geeringh, it's not an idea anymore. It's a business in germination. What will it need to grow? Hard work. Research. Passion. And money.

Typically, Deloitte will spend around US$100 000 on a business case-study, if all the signs and processes show that the return on investment will be worth it. If that does happen – because this is business, not philanthropy – what's in it for the author of the idea? Glory, self-esteem, recognition. And money.

"On a monthly basis," says Geeringh, "we'll reward the person who contributed the best idea with a bonus of US$5 000 or more. But if it's a great idea that allows us to start generating serious profit, there's no limit to what we'll pay out. No limit at all. Our global leaders are committed to paying hundreds of thousands of dollars for successful new businesses."

Naturally, such ideas are few and far between. As soon as you create an open forum for new business opportunities, particularly with such a handsome incentive at its core, you're going to find yourself dealing with an unusually high ratio of noise to signal.

Geeringh admits: "However a bad idea can turn out to be a not-so-bad idea when you start applying some thought to it. But our problem is that we simply don't have enough bandwidth for the volume of ideas that come in. The real value of the process lies in

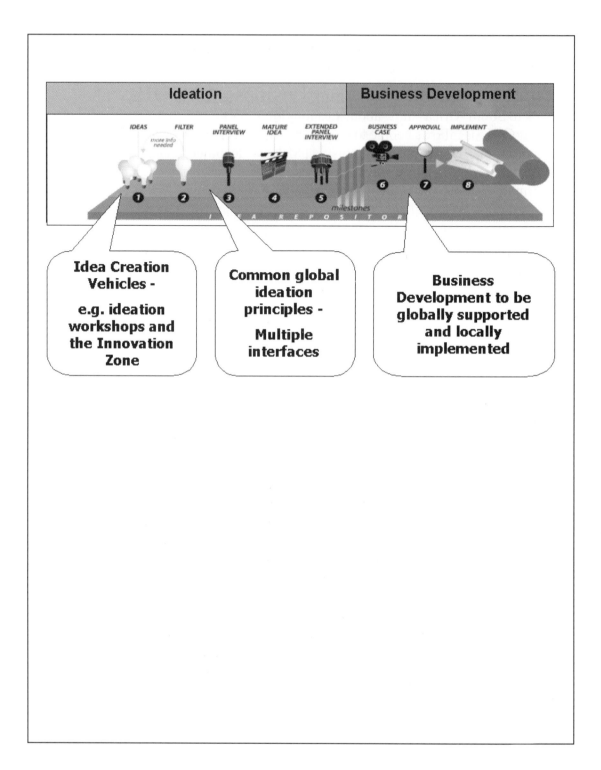

the business development side. And that's where our pipeline is limited and where our core focus is."

Think. Think Deloitte. Think business. Think big.

Back to South Africa – how about an anonymous hotline – call it Tip-Offs Anonymous – that allows people to report unethical or criminal behaviour in an organisation? How about a sophisticated legal document management system – let's call it Lexicon – that allows you to keep track of the avalanche of information that flows in with every new deal, every new contract? How about a similar system, called ShareTrust, that allows company secretaries to tame the paper-trail of share options for employees?

There you have three ideas that made it through the process, three ideas that made – and are making – money for Deloitte & Touche.

"We always say," says Geeringh, "that there are millions of incredible products, millions of incredible pieces of software, just sitting in closets around the world. We'll never know about them, because they'll never be exposed to the light. No matter how good it is, an idea means nothing unless it can be developed and applied commercially."

Once that happens, the idea becomes a virus, self-replicating, radical, unstoppable. Even when the idea itself draws inspiration from a virus of the opposite variety.

Geeringh: "It's about the right people, with the right idea, at the right time."

"This guy comes to see us," says Geeringh, "with an idea for a product that provides updates for antivirus software, via satellite. Instead of having

Setting up the internal venture capital fund

- Create an investment mandate. In addition to the usual issues, such as, maximum investment size, industry split, etc, the mandate include the following:
  - Preferred valuation method
  - Reporting methods (both within the fund and within the investments)
  - Method for assessing the size of the return to match the risk
- Develop a complete reporting structure that is in full compliance with the latest global standards
- Appoint and train fund managers
- Appoint and train Business Mentors
- Train directors and committee members
- Develop governance structures for the fund that will allow the risks to managed in an orderly fashion

Managing the fund

- Identify the tools required to administer the fund:
  - Tool to harvest and screen innovation from across the business – something equivalent to *Innovation Zone*
  - Workflow management tool to the fund's specific requirements – something equivalent to *Venture Catalyst*
- Perform detailed pre-investment screening
- Perform due diligence work.
- Investment management.
- Diagnostic services, for distressed investments and investment exits
- Identify which of the above should be sourced externally

to go to your software provider's website, and download information at the same time as hundreds of thousands of other companies around the globe, you put a decoder on top of your server, and the update arrives without you even knowing it."

Great idea. Simple, transparent, cost-effective. Trouble is, nobody was interested: it was an idea without backing, an idea without support. Until Deloitte, having taken it through every step of the process – interview, analysis, business study – agreed to allow one of its own servers to be used as a test-case.

When an entrepreneur approaches Deloitte the company doesn't show him the door. Well, they do, except it's the door of an office, with a desk and a PC, where he will be free to sit for three weeks, fine-tune his idea, with the entire global Deloitte network at his disposal, and then come into an interview and convince a panel that the seed of a business is ready to be nurtured. Just add money.

And, here's the rub. Just how does a large organisation manage the funds to be allocated for radical innovation? Shareholders want the best returns every quarter and certainly don't want to see a successful business 'squandering' hard earned cash on radical projects with dubious futures.

Managing the funds allocated for innovation within an organisation is becoming as professional a task as the venture capital business has become in the open marketplace. Many large organisations have chosen to outsource this responsibility, and this in turn has become a substantial business for Deloitte Touche Tohmatsu. But it's clear whether you outsource or choose to create an internal investment bank to manage the funds you allocate to radical innovation, the principles and guidelines are the same.

The management and governance of a venture capital fund needs to be clearly defined to ensure that it becomes a well-governed business, generates good returns and achieves strategic economic objectives with the lowest risk to its stakeholders.

"If you do your work properly," says Geeringh, "the process shouldn't distinguish between an internal and an external innovator. The scorecard and the criteria remain the same."

Deloitte Touche Tohmatsu have made radical innovation an integral part of their corporate DNA and now they are encouraging their clients to take

the same radical medicine. They are rolling out customised versions of *Innovation Zone* and *Venture Catalyst* to their clients, creating resonance with the marketplace.

The idea. The people. The feasibility.

If each component passes the test,

the idea gets the green light. Green for go, green for money.

Think. Think R300 million. Think 2001. Did the South African division of Deloitte Touche Tohmatsu manage to close the gap, to live up to its four-year goal of R1,2 billion in revenue?

"No," says Geeringh. "We exceeded the revenue target, even though we're still working on aligning the profitability of our newer businesses with our historic one."

So why has South Africa taken the challenge of leading the innovation efforts of a global firm the size of Deloitte Toche Tohmatsu? "Well," says Geeringh, "most innovation seems to occur at the edge of the empire — away from the controls, the corporate governance and the constraints of the emperor. When all the odds are against you and you have to do things out of neccessity to stay in business, as in the case with South Africa, it breeds a certain type of hunger in people – and essential nutrient to make innovation flourish."

Here's the bottom line. It's not just about money. It's not just about profit. It's about the right people, with the right idea, at the right time, in the right place. Get that formula right, and you're in business.

MY INNOVATION ZONE

Lessons Learnt

Radical business growth can be achieved through setting
out-of-the-box 'unachievable' targets

Given the chance, people come up with a flood of dynamic ideas

Speed of response in assessing and evaluating proposals is key

The right tools make innovation manageable and pervasive

Identify the 'sitting duck' opportunities and develop those first

Internal 'venture capital funds' and 'investment banks' are a
necessary part of the implementation of innovations in large
organisations

Innovation must be driven outside of
day-to-day business processes

New ventures need to be assessed with new rules and nurtured
outside the normal business culture

10

Herding cats

The golden thread that runs through radical innovation

How to **attract** and **retain** the **brightest young things,** and the **implications** of working with them

If you're a fan of cowboy movies – and be honest now, who isn't? – you'll probably have fond memories of an old epic called *Red River*, starring John Wayne and his younger sidekick, Montgomery Clift.

It's about the battle for land, the battle between generations, the battle between the pioneers of the untamed West, and the indigenous tribes who already occupied the territory. But mostly, it's about cattle.

The centrepiece of the story is a long, gruelling trek to drive a herd of more than 6 000 steers northwards across the raging river of the title, and on towards Kansas. There are thunderstorms, sandstorms, gunfights, fistfights, stampedes.

Even if you aren't a fan of cowboy movies, it's a film worth watching, because it seems to say something about the relentless determination, grim resolve, and inexhaustible energy required to get almost any big project on the road. This applies particularly in the world of business.

Substitute budgets for sandstorms, competitors for fistfights, and stock-market listings for stampedes, and you begin to get the picture.

In the preceding chapters of this book, our case studies of radical innovation are characterised by individuals actively driving their organisations away from traditional industrial-age management  – the days of managing people as if we were herding cattle.

First, we'd put each of the vertical smokestack organisations, like administration, marketing and sales, into a different pen. As an employee, you'd be fenced off and actively encouraged not to jump the fence. If you did so, without permission, then you could expect to be punished. The rules were well understood.

The concept that 'Work is what you do, not where you go' had not yet surfaced. It was a world of 9-to-5. You had to be there, in your pen, to be considered to be of value. Every now and then you would see a cowboy on a large horse ride into the adjacent pen and start whipping the cattle into shape.

"Gee, I wonder what they did wrong," you would wonder. The group in your pen would immediately decide to keep a low profile and do as they were told, lest they too be subjected to such punishment. You never questioned your superiors. After all, they knew best.

But that was the old world. Things have changed.

Today staff are actively encouraged to challenge all the hoary old rules. To think independently, and listen to the market.

Sometimes, it seems as if business in an innovative world has become pure anarchy.

In spite of our opening contention that there is no golden bullet for radical innovation, it must have emerged in your subconscious that there is a very strong golden thread running through our stories of radical innovation.

This golden thread is one of unreasonable, restless people, for whom the best is never good enough, for whom there is always a better way. To them there are no imperatives, no rigidly-defined boundaries, no "cattle pens". There are always other ways of seeing the problem. To them, there are opportunities in every business black hole.

These are the people who thrive despite the environment. They capitalise on everything around them, good or bad. They have access to exactly the same resources as others, yet they always seem able to create more value.

They are exactly the kind of people that many good managers hate to have working for them! In fact, it's often said they can't be 'managed'. If

Managing People Is Like Herding Cats
by Warren Bennis

Herding Cats Across the Supply Chain
by Ram Reddy

Herding Cats - Multiparty Mediation in a Complex World
edited by Chester A. Crocker

managing a business was like 'herding cattle', then this is the equivalent of 'herding cats'.

The phrase has come into common usage in high technology circles to describe the difficulty of managing the seemingly unmanageable. Just look at the titles of some recent business books and articles at left.

Yes, everyone's talking about the challenge of herding cats. And at the heart of the dilemma, we find a classic Generation Gap: most of the 'herders' will be people in their 40's and 50's, while most of the 'cats' will be twentysomethings. It's the Baby Boomers versus the Generation Xers. Different points of view, different sets of values.

As a 'Baby Boomer' of the Woodstock generation, you will probably find little difficulty managing other Boomers: "Anything's possible. Let's get out there and do it!". You may even have become resigned to the fixation on security and loyalty so characteristic of your parent's generation – the so-called Silent Generation. But now, the bright young people you are trying to attract into business are just not playing the game. They don't seem to play by the same rules, they don't have the same values. And yet, you are completely dependent on their energy, drive and technical skills.

All the more so in an organisation driven by the radical innovation imperative.

Aletha Ling, one of the young veterans of the rollercoaster DotCom world, is a person who knows a bit about these young 'cats', and the difficulty of creating an organisation around them.

In 1995, Ling and partner Anne Czerner, created waves in the South African computer industry by leaving IBM and starting a highly successful software solutions business, Software Futures.

Software Futures quickly captured the imagination of the market. Within just three years, the company reached a market cap of more than R100 million. Naturally, with the insatiable demands for cash inherent in high growth companies, they became the target of an increasingly acquisitive market. They were acquired by CCH in a classical cash plus shares deal where the shares dominated. The innovative Software Futures was now part of a much bigger entity. Different priorities, different cultures, different principles.

The subsequent failing fortunes of CCH have become the stuff of legend.

Without knowing it,
Ling had stepped into quicksand.

As the group spiralled downwards on the back of poor publicity and worse press coverage, Ling was appointed Group CEO in an attempt to pull the company out of its dive. At this stage it seems there was nothing that could come between CCH and the inevitable. At a late stage, with the share price at just 5% of its peak just two years before, Aletha led the acquisition of the company by MGX.

In a heady period of less than 3 years, Ling's fortunes had fluctuated wildly. She had **experienced** the leadership **equivalent** of a **journey** to **hell and back.** Who said that radical innovation was easy?

She reflects: "We built Software Futures around three key tenets: Radical Innovation, Breakthrough Implementation and Thought Leadership. We believed these would translate into serious value for our clients, but we knew they would have to be built on a very different business model and with very different people.

"Our industry – Information Technology – has changed a lot. It's fundamentally about very talented people, professionals who don't suffer fools gladly, and who have great freedom of choice when it comes to deciding who they want to work for. Being a leader in such an organisation requires a very different mindset from that of ten years ago.

Ling: A life on the rollercoaster

"To create the environment for **growth** and **innovation** we created something called the **'spinout model'**, and what it entailed was creating a leadership environment that would make room for a new, younger breed of individual. "The spinout model was devised to encourage entrepreneurship by allowing ideas to surface, and then giving free rein to the individual with the passion and ability to turn the idea into a successful venture. This is the 'white space' required for radical innovation. It was in

Lessons from the rollercoaster

When there is less hierarchy of management,
and more philosophy of leadership,
a great deal of trust becomes necessary.

Open communication builds
organisational robustness against outside forces.

The more appropriate the culture,
the more the dream is shared,
the more likely it is that individuals will make good decisions.

While talented young professionals are
typically self-directing, with great skills,
motivation, and drive, they still need to work within a team.

Build companies that can survive in any kind of market –
not just bull markets.

Leaders provide the 'energy' that
drives an organisation.
Leaders must motivate and enthuse,
not by exacting obedience
but by inspiring great performance.

It's easy to succeed in
predictable markets.
In turbulent times, innovation becomes the key
to sustained growth.

fact an early form of what venture capitalists came to call the incubator model, except that it was run inside the company.

"The great thing about this approach is that it allows individuals to think about and conceptualise new ideas, but it also meant that they have to take ownership and responsibility for turning the idea into a real business venture. This, for me, is the difference between dreamers and entrepreneurs. People have to accept real ownership. The declining fortunes of CCH had a real impact on many people. It significantly changed the environment in which Software Futures operated."

What are the lessons Aletha Ling has learned from her rollercoaster experience? Take a look at the summary at left.

"Get this right, and herding cats becomes a pleasure and a joy, rather than a chore."

Would she do it all again?

As a serial innovator, Aletha Ling probably knows no other way. Today, as Strategy Executive of MGX, Aletha is taking great pleasure in innovating and helping her new company grow into the future.

But it's one thing to herd cats and strive for innovation in a company that stands at the forefront of the IT revolution.

Ling... the joy of herding cats

It's quite another when you're running an organisation whose main line of business just happens to be herding cattle. Or at least, herding cars, trucks, boats, planes, trains, freight, and commuters.

How do you innovative, how do you herd cats, when you're running the biggest parastatal in the land?

Let's talk to Mafika Mkwanazi, managing director of Transnet. Here we have a company where authority is cautiously delegated, and where the

consequences of failure can result in powerful public censure.. Even so, Mkwanazi recognises the need to provide 'white space' for people to explore.

Transnet MD Mkwanazi

"As a small boy I would lug heavy boxes of peanuts and handkerchiefs to sell to train passengers on the Faraday line between Soweto and Johannesburg".

Back at home, Mafika, the youngest of four children, would light a candle at night, then read and study into the early hours, an effort that kept him in the top five in his school.

"I will never forget where I came from. Yes, there was poverty, but my mother gave me the greatest gift – the space and support to do whatever I wanted to do."

He is now applying that thinking to the future of Transnet, breaking up the unwieldy conglomerate into smaller focused business entities with private sector involvement in each one. "In five years I want to see just ten people in Transnet head office, just a core of people managing the investments and leaving the businesses to focus on what they do best. This transition will not be easy, we will need to bridge the generational and ideological divide. We must give more space to the operating companies, allow them to be viable and thrive."

But a South African reality is that most of our young people will not find jobs in the corporate world. Mafika himself has a teenaged son and daughter. What would his advice be to them?

"I would encourage them to see themselves as global workers, to develop the specific skills that are valued globally and to get into that growing job market."

True to his word, he has involved Transnet in training youngsters to capitalise on the global market, for example by funding a maritime training institute, which will help develop skills that are in short supply world wide.

"We have to focus our innovations at the vast global market".

What **Mafika's mother** intuitively gave to her **youngest** child is what **every corporation** ought **to give** to their people –
the space to flourish.

Think about it, would you really build a successful sport team by getting each of your star players to conform? Wouldn't you want each of them to exercise their own particular skill to the utmost? To push the barriers! See how far they can take it!

Similarly, we should not shape our cats to the corporate mould. We should allow each and every one to exercise their unique skills, and let the market be the judge of the value they add.

It takes bold leadership and the courage to allow for risk and failure. To allow for constant criticism of the status quo. To thrive in the uncomfortable environment created by never-satisfied cats. Creating this environment will attract the bright young things, and make the difference between success and failure.

Innovation thrives on open leadership that lives on the edge of chaos and finds inspiration in uncertainty. That's why managing innovation is like herding cats.

If it's so **tough** why even **start** attracting **cats** to your business? **Why** do it **at all?**

EDS, the global IT services firm, ran a wonderful advertising campaign that captured the essence of this idea.

To me, the most powerful concept is in the closing line in the 30 second ad:

"When you bring a herd into town, there ain't a feeling like it in the world!"

Herding cats is not just about the challenges of 'herding' or leading highly talented professionals. Herding cats is ultimately about the rewards – about the pride and satisfaction you feel when you bring the herd into town.

MY RADICAL TO-DO LIST

Lessons Learnt

Thrive on chaos and uncertainty, it's the new way of the world

Get ready to have the cats question every aspect of your business

Capitalise on the diversity of generations

Replace the hierarchy of management,
with a philosophy of leadership

Create an open corporate environment
in which entrepreneurs can thrive

Spin out radical new ventures to create a white space culture

Learn from those who win and those who
step into quicksand

Get ready to herd cats.
There's no feeling like it in the world!

11

Strategic Thinking and Strategic Action™

A process to make your radical future a matter of choice

Ideally, what do you want your business to be? How do you turn bright ideas into commercial realities? How can you choose your business and personal future?

This chapter will introduce you to a **process** that will help you move your business from **inside-out thinking** about your business to **outside-in thinking** about your business.

I'll show you how to stop asking **"What is my business?"** and focus on **"What do I want my business to be?"**

Well, what did you think of the stories of our radical innovators? Inspirational stuff? Scary? Envigorating?

Right now you're probably thinking:

"That's all very well, **but how do I start?"**

Before we commence our journey into radical innovation, before we pass 'Go', let's look at what, in my mind, remains the key prerequisite to radical innovation.

At a macro level, we can start with a kind of 'trick' question, **the answer** to which **will forever determine** how innovative your business can be. So, be **careful** how you answer.

This is the question:

"What is your business?"

Easy isn't it. But think again. What is your value proposition to the marketplace? Not your perception, but your customers' perception. Whatever customers value, they will pay for in direct proportion to the perceived value. Goodness. And, that translates into long-term profits. Don't interpret their 'value' statement as what you *wish* it was.

Ask the market. Ask your customers.

What do your customers perceive to be value?

Listen carefully to the response. Believe it! Act on it!

What is Black and Decker's business? Power tools? Electric drills?

As a non-technical customer I know that their real value proposition to me is simple – it's just 'holes'. Their ads have consistently left me feeling technically challenged. Why do I need to know the number of revolutions per minute of an electric motor when all I need is a 'hole'.

You see, I would suggest that, like me, many customers only see the drill, the drill bits, the extension cords and the associated paraphernalia as an unnecessary hurdle to achieving 'the hole'.

I would suggest to you that from many customers' point of view, their business is just 'holes'.

Think about the organisation you create when your business is defined as 'electric power tools'. You would employ armies of engineers (they may even become your core competency; the most senior of them may even run the business) and you would have a major Research and Development effort into electric motors, materials technology to improve the drill bits and the like.

If your business were defined as 'holes' you might well have a marketing campaign that would not even mention the technical excellence of your products.

How about "Any hole, anywhere, anytime."

That suddenly turns you into a service business rather than a product business.

If that was how your business was defined I would suggest that you would outsource access to all the best technologies for making holes. Drills would not be a core competency. You would create powerful alliances with all those technology and tool providers.

I'm sure that in the foreseeable future it will become common place to use lasers to make perfect holes around the home and office (any hole anywhere, anytime) without any fuss at all. Today lasers are already so effective and powerful that they can remove layers one molecule thick from your cornea. The price of lasers is falling at a similar rate to microprocessors. How long do you think it will be before these lasers are small and cheap enough to be sold as disposable DIY tools – and make the most perfect holes you have ever seen?

How about buying 'a hole in a box'.

I guess it would most likely be a six-pack of holes. A disposable laser pack containing six holes, 3 mm wide and 12 mm deep.

What about other new technologies such as ultra sound? The typical problem is that any business so focused on improving an existing technology (e.g. 'power tools') may actually miss these new threats and opportunities simply because they fall outside the traditional focus of 'what our business is!' These new innovations may even be seen as 'competitive' – to be understood and fought against!

The moment the answer to the question "What is my business?" changes, then suddenly these peripheral new technologies give you the opportunity to redefine your business. You might change from a 'product focused' business to one focused on 'relationships' or 'solutions'.

When you consider that almost any 'product' business tends to become commoditised as it reaches maturity (characterised by increasing efficiency, more competitors and falling prices) the best business to be in is 'relationships', 'services' and 'solutions'. This is where the customer typically attaches high 'value' and from which you can attract 'profit' in the long-term.

There are of course many businesses that have asked the "What is our business?" question and come up with a surprising answer. What should be interesting to us is that so few businesses have acted boldly on the answer.

Perhaps an even more telling question is "What would we choose our future business to be?"

The Traveller's Tale

A traveller encounters a wise old man in the desert and asks him directions to his destination. The old man looks up at the sky quizzically. He frowns. Then he contemplates the horizon and starts to speak. "Well…" he says, and then stops abruptly. He turns his attention to his feet. Dusty bare feet that have never known shoes. With the wisdom of ages he turns to look the desperate stranger in the eye. Hesitatingly he utters the traveller's worst fears: "If you want to get *there*, then you wouldn't start from *here*."

Given perfect choice, for most companies, it would not be an extrapolation of today's business. Given a clean sheet, given your experience and your knowledge of future markets, would you re-create in the future what you already have today?

Those who have acted radically in response to this question have frequently become widely recognised case studies. Think of global household names such as Nokia (previously a forest products company), and General Electric (a lumbering industrial age giant before Jack Welch turned its profit focus into financial services).

So, what do you choose your future business to be?
Got it?
Now you're ready to think about Radical innovation.

To start with, you have to accept that you'll need to understand the future better than the past!

Radical innovation often succeeds because great entrepreneurs have a lucid anticipation of future markets.

It's always a 'new generation' market out there. Whatever made you successful is by definition already a commodity.

How can you understand the future better than the past?

Over the last fifteen years working to help FutureWorld clients better understand the future we have evolved a process that, like success, has many fathers. I call it Strategic Thinking and Strategic Action™.

The principle behind this way of thinking is that in a market environment that is changing at break-neck speed, the worst place to start contemplating your future is from where you are now.

In a sense, if you want to get to the future, the worst place to start thinking about the future is here, in the present.

You may recall the hoary old story of the lost traveller, as told at left.

Every aspect of the present is in some way derived from the historic baggage of your past. All your past experiences, success and failure, have congealed into what makes you what you are today.

Middle management perceptions of how much of their time top management spends on 'strategy and creating the future', versus 'operating the present'?

How much of their time do you think they **ought to be spending** on 'the future'?	More than 50%
How much of their time do you think they **are spending** on 'the future'?	10 to 30%
The amount of time that **is actually being spent** (based on an analysis of top management diaries).	Less than 10%

So, the first challenge is to separate your thinking about today, from your thinking about the future.

Drawing a thick black wiggly line between your thinking about the present and your thinking about the future is not as easy as it seems.

If you ask any team of managers how much time they think the top management team ought to be spending on creating the future rather than operating the present, the answer is always predictable: "More than they do today."

A straw poll we have frequently done with our clients typically throws up perceptions such as those shown at left.

Isn't it top management's job to create the future of the business? Doesn't the top team appoint middle management to operate the business for them?

When we then analyse a top team's diary we usually find that they spend significantly less than 10% on what is perceived to be their primary role in the business – creating the future.

Consider management behaviour during an average business day or business meeting. We delight in reporting actual numbers and extrapolating them into short term plans. We talk about results and customer satisfaction ratings with passion. If a client call comes in complaining about some operational issue then the executive team jumps to it! We love it! It's where we feel most comfortable. We are all the business equivalent of action heroes.

The most creative of strategic thoughts can be drowned by the flow of operational crises.

It's almost as if the future isn't really all that important. Consider who should really be running the operations of the business. As an executive, didn't you hire a really top person to do that for you? Let them do it! Don't meddle. As an executive you should be focusing more than half your time, energy and wisdom on creating the future of your business.

You know you should. They expect it of you. So why does it not happen?

Years of working with top management teams has led me to one inescapable conclusion: Contemplating the future is the second most unnatural act that you can ask the established executive to perform.

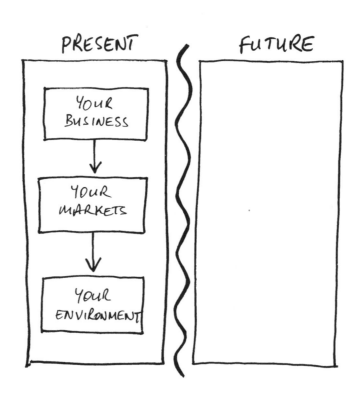

Somehow the here and now is so much more comfortable. We love to be seen to be doing something. Fixing a problem. But be careful.

Never confuse **activity** with **progress.** Especially when it comes to the future.

This dilemma seldom hits young businesses. In an upstart business you're completely focused on building the future business and there is very little current reality to intrude into your passionate dreams about the future. You won't reach this critical stage of the business life cycle until you become successful and your product and customer base grows.

In contrast, think about how most existing, mature businesses spend their average business day. It's almost completely focused on 'our business'. In fact it's primarily an internal view concerned with internal relationships, internal efficiencies, costs, targets, product sales etc.

When we detect problems with meeting some of these targets or the well-oiled business machine is challenged by inputs from the outside ('customer problems', 'crazy new competitors') we are prompted to look externally at the forces threatening the smooth running of the business machine. Typically these are only tended when the noise from outside gets unbearable for those on the inside.

Every now and then, when 'environmental' factors threaten the business (e.g. changes in legislation, dropping of import barriers, changes in labour law or new technologies etc) do we grudgingly take the time to consider their impact. Even so, most of this energy is focused on their current impact – reactive management.

This is how most **established** businesses **focus** on their business – **from the inside out.**

How then can you create a balance between the focus on *today* and *the future*?

The trick is to build an artificial boundary between the present and the future, and focus the mind firmly on the future by constructing a vital and inspiring way to think about the future. This diagram represents that process at a fundamental level.

You have to actively 'ring fence' the process of **contemplating the future**, turn it into a conscious skill and then make it an integral part of your on-going business thinking.

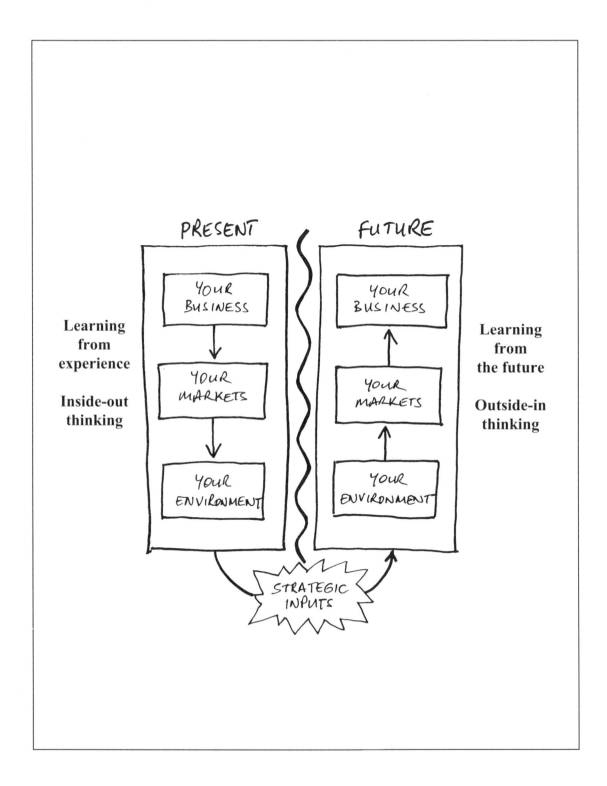

At some point in this process most executive teams have come to the startling but obvious conclusion that you cannot think about the future of your business the same way that you react to the present.

While you may run your business on a day-to-day basis primarily from the inside out, you can only design your future business from the outside in.

The starting point for thinking about the future of your business is not your current business. The best place to start is the future environment. This may be counter-intuitive and it certainly may not appear to fast-track us to a vision for the future, but in a fast-changing marketplace it's the only place to start – by understanding the environment of the marketplace of the future.

Strategic Inputs are the first step in a process we call Learning from the Future. This is the antithesis of the inside-out way of understanding our existing business – this is outside-in thinking.

In this warp-speed world it is simply not enough to learn from experience – you must learn from the future. Let's see how it works in practice.

At first look you might say it's impossible to learn from the future. How can we know it?

Despite the radical changes going on all around us there are some key 'rules of the game' that we can all identify the forces that will be instrumental in shaping our future environment. Also, there are some 'key uncertainties' that could cause the future environment to shape up into two or more possible scenarios. Then there are those 'wild cards' – unlikely but powerful events that could destroy the most basic of our assumptions.

technologies that will:
change production processes
change consumer behaviour
open new markets
increase life span
dramatically cut costs of food, drugs etc

political and regulatory actions that will:
change employment practices
raise operating costs
open markets to competition

social trends that will:
create pressure on global companies
build resistance to global brands
give preference to organic and 'green' products
cause consumers to exercise their individual and group power

This is where our series of **Strategic Inputs** come in. We establish with our clients what they expect the key factors to be that will shape their business environment in the future. A typical list of these is shown at left.

The list can be endless and should be focused on your business priorities and based on answers to the following questions:

What is it about the future that will create positive or negative changes for business?

What are those things we know that we don't know enough about?

What are those things we don't know that we don't know about?
(This dilemma is best answered by staying close to your markets and the youngest brightest people in your business)

We then line up top experts and visionaries to explore each of these issues with them in a series of Strategic Inputs – powerful explorative presentations followed by 'So what?' debates. We ask: "What if what we have just heard does happen? What will be the implications for markets? What new opportunities will be created? What will customers 'value'? What will be the implications for our business in the future?"

Our experts or 'gurus' are all briefed to discuss their area of specialty in a *future perfect* tense (for more on this approach read Stan Davis' classic book *FuturePerfect*).

The FutureWorld Network of Gurus... designing the future

In each of their areas of specialty we begin to
imagine the future as if it has already happened.

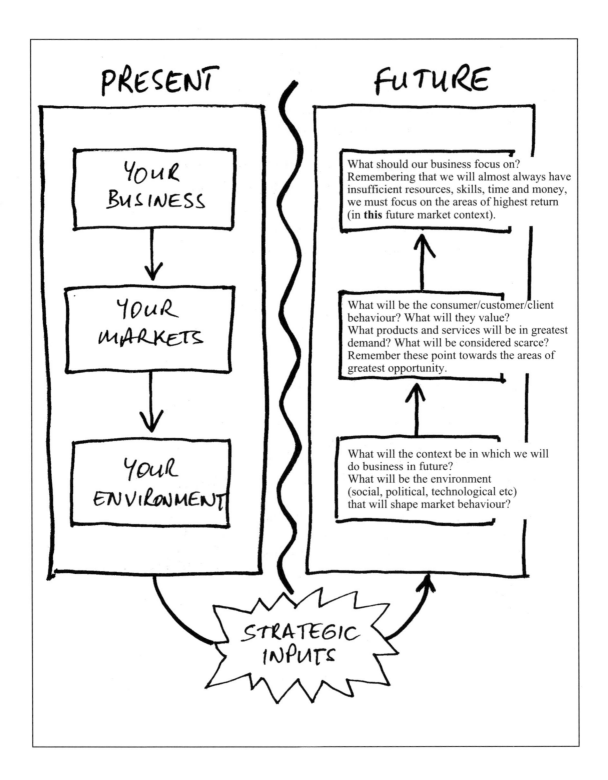

Imagining the future is really a three step process as shown at left.

It's only when you understand the future market context that you can design your desired role within it.

And, if you have the chance to design your future, why design anything less than your ideal future?

Detail is important in both the *understand* and *design* phase. What are we doing? What cars are we driving? How are consumers behaving? Who are our competitors? You have to be able to feel and touch the future.

What started out as a process of Divergent Thinking, based on a challenging series of Strategic Inputs, now turns into a process of Convergent Thinking working towards a series of Strategic Actions.

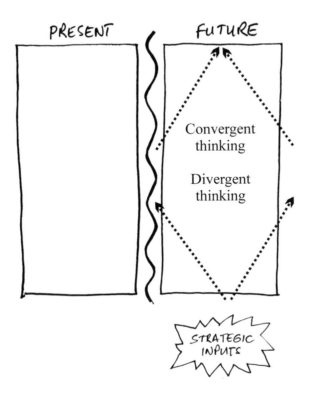

Having debated all the possibilities in the environment, markets and business opportunities, we now have to choose a future for our business.

This is a debate and the outcome is anything but certain. The trick is to consider all the different views of the future, no matter how divergent. We literally have to thrash it out.

If everyone agrees – you know you're on the wrong track. Someone's not thinking clearly. Someone's missed the radical opportunity.

The scary thing is that at this stage, where you are contemplating a really radical opportunity, all the tried and trusted analytical approaches do not help a jot. Market research is useless if the markets don't yet exist. It is folly to ask consumers about radical future products that they cannot even imagine. You'll remember what happened when Sony asked consumers if they had a need for the Walkman, or when early PC pioneers tried to encourage people to think about computers at home. Whatever would we do with them?

However, perfect choice about the future still means that the group has to converge around one ideal future as the basis for their thinking. What one vision for this business can we all feel united and passionate about?

This is not to say that the real future does not have various scenarios. The scenario planning process recognises that there are a number of possible future scenarios for the environment, markets and of course for your business. The whole field of scenario planning is best handled using other publicly available sources. In practice, in my work with FutureWorld and their clients, I have found the need to create a powerful pragmatic approach to short circuit the time consuming processes typically associated with scenario planning.

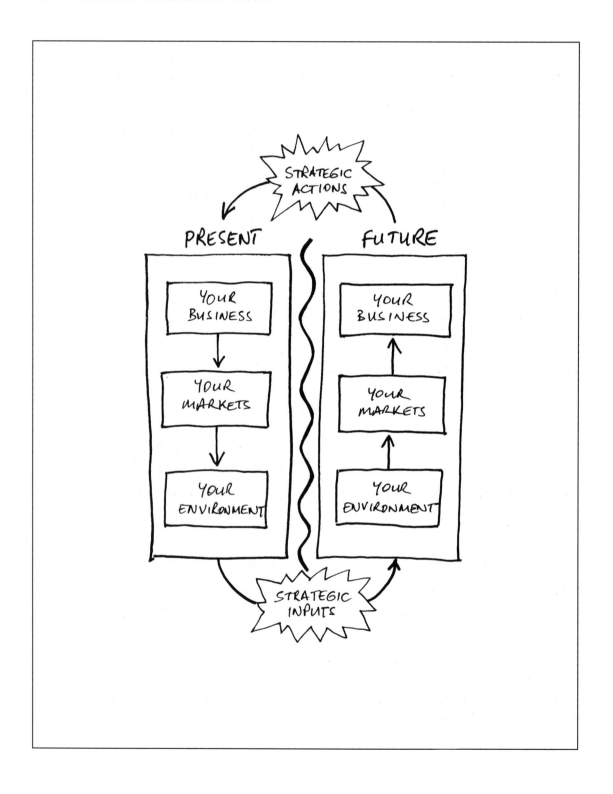

We call our approach 'Strategic Action Scenarios™' and it allows an executive team to see and explore the inter-relationships of the various factors influencing the future in an extremely graphical way. One of the outputs of this process can typically be a 3D structure like this, in this example creating 8 possible future scenarios from which the team can choose one 'scenario of choice' to serve as the basis for Strategic Thinking:

Strategic Action Scenarios ™

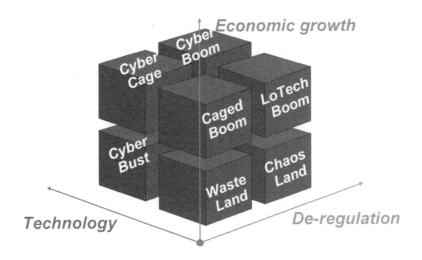

But, first let's go back to a summary of the Strategic Thinking and Strategic Action™ process.

Once we have developed our passionate vision for the future, we need to plant our feet firmly in this future and look back from whence we came:

"Gee isn't this 'future' great. I'm really proud to be a part of this thriving business. But, looking back five years, how did we ever get here? What were the Strategic Actions we took back then to create this reality?"

You see, Strategic Actions are never actions we take in the future. Strategic Actions are those we take today, to create our ideal future.

Do not take this shortcut to your future!

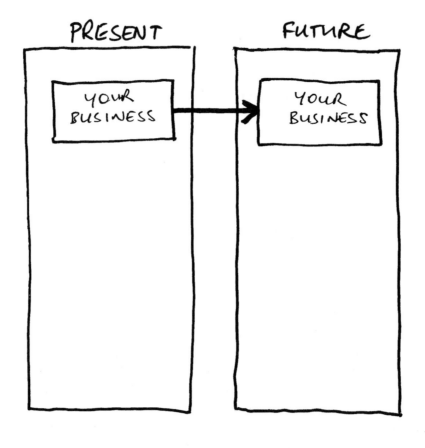

This process does more than define the gap between our future reality and the current reality of the past. It shows us how we bridged the gap. It helps us identify the imperative for Strategic Actions.

It's so much easier and more effective to do this thinking in a future perfect tense. No one can argue that it can't be done. It has been done and that's all there is to it. Now, doesn't it feel great?

Look at the diagram at left. Whatever you do, do not try to contemplate your future this way!

In my experience, when we try to create a view of the future by extrapolating from our past success and where we are today, we fall horribly short of ideal.

We are encumbered by all our own current paradigms of the future. We know why things won't work and justify to ourselves that the really difficult stuff is really not worth the effort. Just think of all the people you will have to win over. Just think of all the politics. Let's just go for something a little more modest.

Allow me to paraphrase Charles Handy who explained the dilemma brilliantly:

"We are walking backwards into the future, with our eyes firmly fixed on our past achievements".

We are literally blinded by the past.

As individuals and as a business we must turn around and look the future squarely in the face! Resist the temptation of romantic dreams about the way things were and what made us so successful in the past.

In order to innovate radically, you must learn to learn from the future!

We have found that Strategic Thinking and Strategic Action™ is a pragmatic process for creating the foundations for radical innovation.

Try it yourself.

evolutionary	radical
Telephone	Mobile phone
Banks	Non-banks
Retail	eTail
Transport	Logistics
Education	Learning
Hardware/Software	Solutions
Chemical	BioTech
Pharmaceutical	Life Sciences
Computer software	The software of living things
Manufacturing physical stuff	Networking information

This can be a fully inclusive process in which all the bright young things in your business can participate. It's a process which can also give you the opportunity to bring your business partners, suppliers and customers actively into the process of choosing your future.

With Strategic Thinking and Strategic Action™ you can build an idealised view of your future that will create a powerful context for radical innovation and the thought leadership you need to harness the bright stuff in your business.

You too can choose your future, together.

And why stop after doing it within your business? Try it with your family! Remember, you are what you do.

If the preceding chapters have taught us anything, it is that radical innovation powerfully lays the foundations for new markets and future growth.

Just check out these industries, their attitudes to innovation and consider which you believe will thrive in the new global context. While there are always exceptions to the rule, I've taken the opportunity to categorise these industries in the table at left.

Just think about how the mobile phone industry has innovated customers away from the traditional telephone industries – all in less than a decade! That's radical innovation at many levels.

In the US, for years now, the primary innovators in banking services have not been the banks. Almost every type of company has muscled into their turf – from auto manufactures and retailers to electricity companies. Some say that more than 90% of new banking services now come from non-banks.

In retailing, the realisation has dawned that competition is no longer between products (they're commoditised and available through everyone) but between business models. Many retailers are turning large chunks of their business into eTail operations. A merger between a WalMart and an Amazon.com may still be a win-win deal for both parties.

Hardware and software companies, always the darlings of investors in the first half of the industry life cycle, are turning to solutions and services business to regain lost profitability. They are turning to what the marketplace now sees as 'value'. IBM, having made that decision in the early 1990's, clearly has a massive first mover advantage here.

Life Sciences and Biotech firms are the radical innovators today and many traditional players in Chemicals and Pharmaceuticals are transforming their conglomerates to align them with the new opportunities for innovation and growth.

As these industries discover the power of the 'software of living things' and further explore the possibilities of the human, animal and plant genomes, they will become the most dramatic growth industry of the 21st Century. For more on these developments read my previous book *Ten Lessons from the Future.*

Look for the telltale signs of evolutionary innovation, evolution focused on products and services in your own business and in your markets. Use the Creative Destruction matrix in Chapter 1 to create an innovation profile for your business.

Ask yourself: Which of the above industries would you rather be a part of? The answer depends on your personal appetite for risk!

Ask yourself: Which industries will have the biggest growth in the long term? Which industries would you invest in for the long-term?

If you chose evolutionary innovation...

After 600 million years of evolutionary innovation…

…you would still be an echinoderm.
In a dark swamp of a market somewhere.
Nobody would know you anymore.
Alive but not thriving.

However, if you chose **radical innovation...**
After just a few years you could become…
…a dominant new species,
…the Tiger Woods of your industry,
or one of *Fortune's* Top Companies!

If you did achieve this...how would you feel?
Energised? Yes. Fulfilled? Certainly. Resonant? You'd feel it!
Exhausted? Without doubt!

But, most of all, you'd probably feel Proud!

In the words of Heather Small's inspirational song *Proud*, let's sum up the personal challenges of radical innovation.

Look into the window of your mind.
Reflect on the fears you've left behind.
Step out of the ordinary.
Feel your soul ascending.
I'm on my way.
Can't stop me now.
And you can do the same.
What have you done today,
to make you feel proud?

And, ultimately, isn't that exactly what radical success is all about?
At the **heart** of these **lessons** in **radical innovation** are **bold** visionary **individuals** who are proud of what they've created.

Radical innovation is driven through the 'unreasonable' behaviour of individuals, typically those who end up becoming the heroes of the revolution.

Without personal **passion**, the **cows** of radical innovation don't calve!

MY CANVAS OF POSSIBILITIES

Lessons Learnt

Step 1:
Nail down what you think you are today!

Step 2:
Consider the changing context of your future
– apply divergent thinking to the environmental and market factors
driving future customer needs and behaviour

Step3:
Design your futures so you can touch and feel the options
– apply convergent thinking around a preferred future

Step 4:
Choose your ideal future and feel how it feels

Step 5:
Ask – how did we get here?
Identify the strategic actions you took to get to your ideal future

Step 6:
Step back into today and
kick off those essential strategic actions – do it now!

Step 7:
Create your future

Step 8:
Enjoy it and you'll thrive in it!